CAMBRIDGE LIBRARY COLLECTION

Books of enduring scholarly value

Art and Architecture

From the middle of the eighteenth century, with the growth of travel at home and abroad and the increase in leisure for the wealthier classes, the arts became the subject of more widespread appreciation and discussion. The rapid expansion of book and periodical publishing in this area both reflected and encouraged interest in art and art history among the wider reading public. This series throws light on the development of visual culture and aesthetics. It covers topics from the Grand Tour to the great exhibitions of the nineteenth century, and includes art criticism and biography.

The Book of Old Edinburgh

This work was first published in 1886 to accompany one of the more eccentric displays at the Edinburgh International Exhibition of the same year. Historically accurate reconstructions of noteworthy but long-demolished Edinburgh buildings were built side by side to create a fictional street. This guide provided visitors with key historical information relating to the recreated buildings and monuments ranging from the medieval market cross to the historic tolbooth. Fact is combined with anecdote, situating the buildings in the wider context of Edinburgh's rich history. The text was written by John Charles Dunlop and Alison Hay Dunlop, antiquarian siblings little known beyond their Edinburgh circles. Of particular interest are the illustrations by William Fergusson Brassey Hole (1846–1917), who later painted the murals in the entrance hall of the Scottish National Portrait Gallery.

T0370914

Cambridge University Press has long been a pioneer in the reissuing of out-of-print titles from its own backlist, producing digital reprints of books that are still sought after by scholars and students but could not be reprinted economically using traditional technology. The Cambridge Library Collection extends this activity to a wider range of books which are still of importance to researchers and professionals, either for the source material they contain, or as landmarks in the history of their academic discipline.

Drawing from the world-renowned collections in the Cambridge University Library and other partner libraries, and guided by the advice of experts in each subject area, Cambridge University Press is using state-of-the-art scanning machines in its own Printing House to capture the content of each book selected for inclusion. The files are processed to give a consistently clear, crisp image, and the books finished to the high quality standard for which the Press is recognised around the world. The latest print-on-demand technology ensures that the books will remain available indefinitely, and that orders for single or multiple copies can quickly be supplied.

The Cambridge Library Collection brings back to life books of enduring scholarly value (including out-of-copyright works originally issued by other publishers) across a wide range of disciplines in the humanities and social sciences and in science and technology.

The Book of
Old Edinburgh

And Hand-Book to the 'Old Edinburgh Street'
Designed by Sydney Mitchell, Architect,
for the International Exhibition
of Industry, Science, and Art,
Edinburgh, 1886

JOHN CHARLES DUNLOP
ALISON HAY DUNLOP
ILLUSTRATED BY WILLIAM HOLE

CAMBRIDGE
UNIVERSITY PRESS

CAMBRIDGE
UNIVERSITY PRESS

University Printing House, Cambridge, CB2 8BS, United Kingdom

Published in the United States of America by Cambridge University Press, New York

Cambridge University Press is part of the University of Cambridge.
It furthers the University's mission by disseminating knowledge in the pursuit of
education, learning and research at the highest international levels of excellence.

www.cambridge.org
Information on this title: www.cambridge.org/9781108066266

This edition first published 1886
This digitally printed version 2013

ISBN 978-1-108-06626-6 Paperback

VIEW IN 'OLD EDINBURGH' STREET.

THE BOOK OF
OLD EDINBURGH

And Hand-Book to the

OLD EDINBURGH STREET

Designed by SYDNEY MITCHELL, Architect

For the International Exhibition of Industry, Science, and Art
EDINBURGH, 1886

With Historical Accounts of the Buildings therein reproduced
and Anecdotes of Edinburgh Life in the Olden Time

BY JOHN CHARLES DUNLOP AND
ALISON HAY DUNLOP

Illustrated by WILLIAM HOLE, A.R.S.A.

Printed by T. & A. CONSTABLE, Printers to Her Majesty
at the INTERNATIONAL EXHIBITION
EDINBURGH, 1886

𝕿𝖍𝖊 𝕭𝖔𝖔𝖐 𝖔𝖋 𝕺𝖑𝖉 𝕰𝖉𝖎𝖓𝖇𝖚𝖗𝖌𝖍

IS DEDICATED TO

THE MOST HON. THE

MARQUESS OF LOTHIAN, K.T.

President

TO THE RIGHT HON. THOMAS CLARK

Lord Provost of the City of Edinburgh

Acting Vice-President

TO JAMES GOWANS, Esq.

Lord Dean of Guild

Chairman of the Executive Council

AND TO THE

'OLD EDINBURGH' COMMITTEE OF

THE INTERNATIONAL EXHIBITION

OF INDUSTRY, SCIENCE, AND ART

EDINBURGH 1886.

'OLD EDINBURGH' COMMITTEE

(*As Elected*)

ROBERT SOMERVILLE.	WILLIAM M'EWAN.
PETER MILLER.	ROBERT SHILLINGLAW.
WILLIAM ADAMSON.	DR. JAMES SIDEY.
J. A. BUTTI.	RICHARD CAMERON.
WILLIAM MORRISON.	CAPTAIN HENDERSON.
CUMBERLAND HILL.	WILLIAM COOK.

DAVID CUTHBERT, S.S.C., and JOHN CHARLES DUNLOP, *Conveners*.

LIST OF GIFTS TO 'OLD EDINBURGH.'

BY THE CITY,
Ancient Oak Door.

By JAMES BALLANTINE & SON, Edinburgh,
Ancient Stained Glass.

By ABERFOYLE SLATE Co., Glasgow,
Old Slates from Aberfoyle.

By ANDREW SLATER, Canongate,
Ancient Oak Door.

By J. RITCHIE & SON, Edinburgh,
Turret Clock, with Chimes of four Bells, for the Spire of Nether-Bow Port.

CONTRACTORS FOR 'OLD EDINBURGH.'

GEORGE GILROY & Co., Builders, Edinburgh.
MACFARLANE & WALLACE, Painters, Edinburgh.
WILLIAM ANDERSON & SONS, Military Tailors, Edinburgh.
(*for Dress of the Old Town Guard*).

Prefatory Note.

WHEN requested by the Executive Council of the first Scottish International Exhibition to write a Descriptive Catalogue of the Old Edinburgh Street of the Exhibition, the honour and trust so unanimously accorded were frankly accepted.

Labour was involved, but—the labour was congenial.

A Descriptive Catalogue was partly written when the idea—always latent—gathered strength, that a purely antiquarian and technical description of the buildings was suited only to a special and limited class of readers.

The desire awoke to give each house its own place in Edinburgh history; to people each, so far as possible, with its old inhabitants; or, at least, to note some of the side-lights which are thrown on great events in Scottish history by anecdote, and by observation of the habits and customs, the thought and speech, the dress and demeanour, of those who trod the streets of our native city long ago, and called them *theirs* with as much pride and affection as we do now.

In the writing of this extended plan of the book my sister associated herself with me.   The necessity for compression was great, and the time for the ceaseless verification necessary was short.   No one can be more conscious of the failings and shortcomings of the 'Book of Old Edinburgh' than its authors, but they have done—what in honour and kindliness they were bound to do—their best.

Acknowledgement of thanks is due to Robert Adam, Esq., City Chamberlain, and to the Rev. J. Mercer Dunlop of Pollokshaws, for willing aid given in antiquarian literary research.

JOHN CHARLES DUNLOP,
Convener, Old Edinburgh Committee.

32 CLARENCE STREET,
   April 18, 1886.

Contents.

Illustrations.

The Illustrations have been reproduced by Wm. Watson, Alexander Brown, and John Murray, all of Edinburgh.

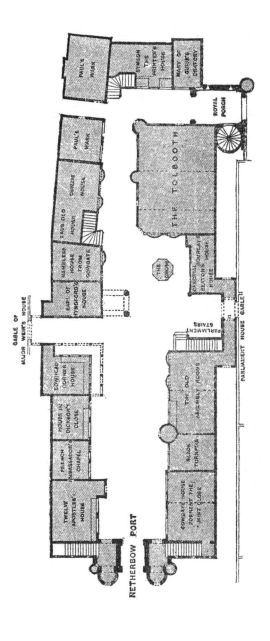

GROUND PLAN OF THE 'OLD EDINBURGH' STREET.

VIEW IN 'OLD EDINBURGH' STREET.

Introduction.

IN the first International Exhibition in Scotland it was thought good to have a representation of ' Old Edinburgh.' Competitive designs were sought and sent in. On the 27th October 1885 the Committee of ' Old Edinburgh' met, and unanimously chose the design marked ' Tolbooth,' and recommended it with confidence for the approval of the General Executive Council. In moving the Report, the Convener of ' Old Edinburgh' said: ' It is only due to the various architects who have competed, to say that the designs were all beautiful, and to tender to them the thanks of the Committee. I have the hope,' he added, ' that the labours of the unsuccessful may not be in vain, for the designs so display the beauty and the unvarying unsameness of Scottish Architecture, that I trust one of the early results of this first great Scottish Exhibition will be a return to a style of building at once suited to the varied scenery and the changeful skies of Scotland, and to the character and history of the Scottish people.'

A

To pass to the successful design:—'Tolbooth' was the competition *nom de plume* of Mr. Sydney Mitchell, well known in these later days as the architect in the restoration of the ancient Market Cross of Edinburgh, Mr. Gladstone's gift to the capital of Scotland.

There is a beautiful verse in the Bible which Dr. John Brown ('Rab') prefixed to one of his exquisite essays: 'I praised the dead which are already dead, more than the living which are yet alive.' This is the underlying charm of our architect's design. No one wanted to see the representation of old Scottish Architecture where the reality still exists, or to see a semblance of John Knox's house, or of Allan Ramsay's house, when the veritable buildings can still be seen by taking a walk down the High Street. The buildings chosen to form the 'Old Edinburgh Street' in the Exhibition, and of which the erections there are a faithful reproduction, have all passed away.

There are certain old titles in the Union Peerage Roll of Scotland that are extinct—honoured and once-powerful families that have dwindled out and died, or that vanished in the hideous ruin that followed upon the Stewart rebellions. The buildings now represented in the Old Edinburgh of the Exhibition are like these extinct peerages. Other historical buildings and other historical families remain, but these have gone to dust. In so far, however, as they were pre-eminently the scenes where the workers in the building up of the National History lived, and laboured, and died, it is good that their memory be thus honoured; for the history there wrought out, though not unstained by feud and faction, and not guiltless of blood and sin, had in it from the earliest times a stern straining to the goal of good—to the light and might of civil and religious liberty, and

> Freedom's battle once begun,
> Bequeathed by bleeding sire to son,
> Though baffled oft, is ever won.

The visitor must note that no specific date can be given for 'Old Edinburgh;' also it goes without saying that the buildings were not contiguous to each other, as now represented; but, though situated in different parts of the ancient city, they had with each other a long contemporaneous existence. The hand of Time, aided by severe conflagrations, and, what was heavier than either, the inroads of our 'auncient innemys of England,' have removed the earlier Edinburgh of Robert Bruce and the Stewart kings. More particularly was this the case with the series of wars, inaugurated in 1544 by Henry VIII., and carried out by his brother-in-law Hertford, to bring about the marriage of the infant Queen Mary of Scots to Edward Prince of Wales. In these inroads Edinburgh suffered severely, and the rebuilding consequent on these devastations has given rise to dis-

crepancies. In the first of these wars the chief city gate
to the east was blown up. The Nether-Bow Port, which
is represented in the Exhibition, and by which the
visitor will enter, was the last of the series—built in
1606 and destroyed in 1764.

To grasp the 'Old Edinburgh' period, it is necessary
to think of the tide of history that has swept through
these successive gates: the earlier Stewart kings,
brilliant, brave, fated; the Reformation Age, with its
actors and workers—Mary of Guise, Cardinal Beaton,
Mary the Beautiful, Darnley, Bothwell, Rizzio, Murray,
Morton, and that one other man who dwarfs all his
contemporaries, John Knox—he who disestablished the
Church of Rome in Scotland, and died without ever
having feared the face of man; then follow the sage
Buchanan, his pupil James vi., and George Heriot,
whose I distribute chearfully has come down all the
Edinburgh generations; then Charles i.; the last sad
entry of Montrose; Cromwell with his stern but im-
partial rule; the Restoration times of the later Stewarts;
the great Argyll and the unyielding martyrs of the
Covenant; then the glorious Revolution; the pioneers of
Scottish emigration in the Darien Scheme, so energetic,
so hopeful, so doomed; the times of Queen Anne and
the Union; the Georgian era; the Rebellion of the '15,
Sheriffmuir, and the Standard on the Braes of Mar; and
the Rebellion of the '45 under Prince Charlie—the last

of his race who entered the northern capital as a gated and a walled city.

This may be held to be the boundary line of the Old Edinburgh' period, for the destruction of the Nether-Bow Port synchronises with the foundation of the New Town on the heathy moor of the Lang Gait in the earlier years of the reign of George III.

The buildings in the 'Old Edinburgh' of the Exhibition are the buildings of Edinburgh within her gates and walls; and in that earlier Edinburgh every stone, almost every step, is historical. Besides her dower of beauty, the Capital of the North has ever possessed an individuality more marked than that of any other city in the Empire. Much of this may be owing to the nature of the country and the character of the people; but very much is due to the genius of Sir Walter Scott, 'her chiefest scribe and recorder,' who has revealed the strong lights and the dark shadows of Scottish story, as with a Rembrandt light, to a reading world.

To that reading world, from the north to the farthest south, and from the east to the most distant west, we offer some representation of the scenes where that Scottish History was lived and enacted; for in so far as that history was pure and honest, fearlessly God-fearing and true, it has given our country its place among the nations.

Nether-Bow Port.

IN the extended city wall, called the 'Flodden Wall,'
there were six principal gates. The chief of these
was the Nether-Bow Port, which separated the city of
Edinburgh from the burgh of the Canongate, at the
conjunction of Leith Wynd and St. Mary's Wynd. It
was the principal entrance to the city from the east,
more especially London, and from the seaport Leith by
Leith Wynd. The King's highway continued to be by
the Canongate and the High Street till the new eastern
approach by the Regent Arch was opened in 1817.
There were three successive Nether-Bow Ports. There
are no representations of the two earlier gates, but
we know that the second was thirty yards nearer John
Knox's house than the last of the series, which was taken
down on 9th August 1764, the material being sold by
public auction.

This building was very massive, and was one of the
greatest adornments of the city. It is said to have
been almost a duplicate of the ancient Porte St. Honoré
at Paris, and it is not unlike some of the old city
gates in Holland. The bell was cast at Campvere

6

in Zealand at the same time as the bells of St Giles'. The successive Nether-Bow Ports sustained a very important part in the city's history, both in the pageants of peace connected with the state entry of the different Stewart sovereigns into the capital, and also in the manifold international wars and city 'tuilzies.'

The Porteous Mob in 1736 had nearly settled the doom of the Nether-Bow Port. The Go-

NETHER-BOW PORT.

vernment, enraged at the insult offered to Queen Caroline's Regency while the King was absent in Hanover, offered large rewards for the apprehension of the ringleaders. Enraged at their non-success, a Bill was introduced into the House of Commons, in which, amongst other pains and penalties against town and magistrates, there was one clause, to dismantle the Nether-Bow Gate and disband the Town Guard. The Scottish Members in London stood shoulder to shoulder, encouraged by the example of John, Duke of Argyll, who, in the House of Lords, denounced in no measured words the intended

WITH YOUR MAJESTY'S LEAVE, TO GET MY BEAGLES READY.

degradation to the ancient capital of Scotland. 'I will make Scotland a hunting-field,' said the angry Queen. 'Then,' said the Duke, 'I go down, with

your Majesty's leave, to get my beagles ready.' The
stately courtliness of the words was Delphic, the deep
reverence of the bow was ominous.   Could the name
of Argyll be dissevered from the cause of the Protestant succession in spite of his family wrongs?   There
was a skeleton at the Court feasts of the second George,
as at those of Egypt long ago.   Was there not growing up at Rome a young prince of the exiled Stewart
race — brave, spirited, debonair?   What were his
possibilities against those of the king's Fritz?   Stolen
waters were not unsweet to the statesmen of the period.

The issues were
weighty. The Go-
vernment gave
way, and the mat-
tèr was eventually
commuted into a
money   payment
by the city of
Edinburgh to the
widow of Captain
Porteous.

The after-
echoes of the
storm were amus-

TAKEN BY THE HIGHLANDERS.

ing. Edinburgh was allowed to possess her Nether-
Bow Gates, but they were to be 'cleekit back'—to

stand open by night as well as by day—so that the
city might be scoured through by a detachment of the
British army when the second Porteous Mob came !
Nine years afterwards, and the Nether-Bow Port was
taken in war for the last time, the assailants being the
Highlanders of Prince Charles's army in the Rebellion
of 1745.   There must then have been a rush for neat's-
foot oil and for the hammermen of the good smith craft
of the Magdalen Chapel.   The gates were in bad order.

No wonder !   The succes-
sors of Vulcan in Old
Edinburgh did their work
promptly and well, and
the gates were eventually
closed.   The capture, however, was an easy one.
There is some historical
haze about the transaction,
but—the Provost was a
Stewart.

GATES IN BAD ORDER.

We learn from a table
of the 'Common Good' in
1690 that the rent of the apartments over the Nether-
Bow Gate was £112 Scots[1]—surely, of all houses in
neighbourly Edinburgh, the best for a 'School for
Scandal' or for gossip !   Further, from the 'Funeral

[1] £10 sterling.

Sermon by Claudero' over the old gate's decreed
downfall, we learn that there was a smithy in the Port,
and that the Nether-Bow Coffee-house was literally 'at
the gate,' thus making the old Nether Bow a very
news-centre for all classes of the populace.   The
smithy, doubtless, might be in the Northern Vault,
which was of greater value in 1558, when it was mort-
gaged for 100 merks to repair the whole structure.

A brief extract from the Nether Bow's 'Funeral Sermon' will show Claudero's grim humour; and the sarcastic
prophecy concerning Leith Harbour has happily found
fulfilment.   'What was too hard,' he says, 'for the
great ones of the earth, yea, even queens to effect, is
now, even in our day, accomplished. No patriot Duke
opposeth the scheme as did the great Argyll in the grand
senate of our nation.   Therefore the project shall go into
execution, and down shall Edina's lofty porches be
hurled with a vengeance. . . . The city shall be joined
to Leith on the north, and a procession of wise masons
shall there lay the foundation of a spacious harbour.
. . . Our city shall be the greatest wonder of the
world; and the fame of its glory shall reach the distant
ends of the earth.'

On the final destruction of the Nether-Bow Gate by
the order of the magistrates of Edinburgh, the ancient
clock was placed in the tower of the Old Orphan Hospital, which stood not far from the site of the present

General Post-Office of Edinburgh.   When the Hospita
was removed for the construction of the North Britisl
Railway, the old clock is said to have found an abiding-
place and work in the tower of the New Orphan Hospital at the Dean.   For one hundred and twenty years
has the old Nether-Bow clock told the flight of time to
these love-bereft children ; but never did it look down
on a young face more sad than it did some two hundred years ago, when James VII. was King.   In the first
year of that king's reign the martyr James Guthrie was
executed at the ' Mercat Croce' without the shadow of
a trial, and

> ' They have set his head on the Nether Bow,
>   To scorch in the summer air ;
> And months go by, and the winter's snow
>   Falls white on his thin grey hair.
>
> There sitteth a child by the Nether Bow
>   In the light of the summer sky ;
> And he steals there yet in the winter's snow,
>   But he shuns the passers-by,—
>
> A child in whom childhood's life is dead,
>   Its sweet life marred and dim ;
> And he gazes up at that awful head
>   As though it held speech with him.
>
> But ever he meekly went his way
>   As the stars came o'er the place,
> And his mother wept as she heard him say,
>   "I have seen my father's face." ' '

When, after the old Scottish law fashion, the Doom-
ster had pronounced his doom, Guthrie turned to his
judges and said, 'My Lords, . . . let never my blood
be required of the King's children.'

HE GAZES UP AT THAT
AWFUL HEAD.

The Twelve Apostles' House,

AND THE

French Ambassador's Chapel.

THIS house was situated in the Cowgate, at the foot of Libberton's Wynd. It was taken down in 1829 for the erection of George IV. Bridge, and it was a good example of the semi-fortified Scottish town house. A strong square tower, presenting the appearance of a narrow Border peel, contained a comparatively well-lighted staircase, which was entered by a stout oak door, beautifully and minutely panelled. In the uppermost story of the west wing there was a double dormer window, surmounted by a pediment on which were carved the heads of the Twelve Apostles. On the top was a figure supposed to have been a representation of our Saviour, but the upper part of the body had long been broken away.

Tradition has ascribed to the east wing of this ancient building the name of 'The French Ambassador's Chapel,' and on the first floor above the street a

14

room with two handsome windows was indicated as the
one that had been so used in the short personal reign
of Queen Mary,
from 1561 to
1567. It must
have required
all the sacred-
ness that is
understood to
surround an Am-
bassador's per-
son and belong-
ings to keep this
chapel from dis-
turbance. Stung
by harsh mea-
sures under the
Beatons and the
regency of Mary
of Guise, the
popular idea of
the mob was
that

THE TWELVE APOSTLES' HOUSE.

' The Paip, that Pagan fou o' pride,
    Has troubled us fu' lang,'

and that the time of retribution had now fully come, and
was in their own hands. Above the doorway was a shield

bearing a crescent between two stars in chief, with the motto, 'SPERAVI · ET · INVENI,' but the principal device on the shield was a *Werewolf*—surely the weirdest and the most horrible guardian that ever man placed over his threshold.   This touches on what was once a wide-spread superstition.   *Were* is the Anglo-Saxon *wer*, a man.   A man-wolf, or Werewolf, was a man who either was transformed, or by the help of Satan had the power of transforming himself for a time, into a wolf, becoming possessed of all the passions and appetites of that animal — more particularly a never-satisfiable hunger to feast on human flesh.   As a species of madness the disease is called 'lycan-thropy,' and there are notices of it in Herodotus, Pliny, and other ancient authors.   In Northern and Mid Europe, in the sixteenth and seventeenth centuries, this superstition, and the cruelties consequent thereon, were at their highest.   These were synchronous with the persecutions for witchcraft in our own country (notori-ously in Old Edinburgh) and in New England across the Atlantic.   In the Jura alone, 600 people suffered by their own confession.   The night before the Feast of the Nativity was the Walpurgis Nacht, or the 'Devil's Sabbath at e'en,' for the werewolves.   It seems that Satan's power stopped short of changing the softness of the human eye, and wounds and mutila-tions in the wolf state discovered the wrong-doers on their resumption of the human form. In an old legend, a knight was attacked by a werewolf. Something in the animal's beautiful eyes startled him when its fangs were at his throat. He fought for his life. The werewolf fled, with a long strange cry, leaving its fore-paw on the ground. On it the knight saw the betrothal ring he had given his mistress, who was found the next day dead in her bower, and —without her left hand.

HE FOUGHT FOR HIS LIFE.

In 1572, when such were the tales that were told round the hearths of Old Edinburgh on winter nights—and not disbelieved,—it would be more than a matter of strange coincidence when John Dickison of Winkston, the builder of this house, was murdered on the High Street of Peebles in open day, and his murderers acquitted. Instead

B

of werewolves, this was an age when both religion and superstition, and much that savoured of neither, wanted something good written on their lintels and door-posts, either as a benediction or a protection. Whether inscribed in Latin, or written in homely Saxon Scotch with quaint spelling, there is nothing more pleasant or more refreshing to the eye of the antiquary than the *guid words whilk trew men carvit in stane aboon their doors at hame.*

The most frequent of the Latin inscriptions was—

SOLI · DEO · HONOR · ET · GLORIA.

—the grace after meat used in families of pretension and learning ; and the most popular of all was the early Reformation grace before meat—

BLISSIT · BE · GOD · FOR · AL · HIS · GIFTIS.

The terminating words when used at table were *through Jesus Christ, Amen*—surely the most comprehensive and beautiful of all thanksgivings.

House in Dickson's Close.

DICKSON'S CLOSE is the first close east from Niddry Street on the south side of the High Street. This house, with its stone basement and projecting wood and plaster upper stories, is supposed to have been the work of Robert Mylne, the builder of the modern portion of Holyrood, and the seventh Royal Master Mason of that hereditary builder-craft family. The date of its building was probably about the Revolution era.

In 1508 James IV. granted by charter the Borough Muir to the Town Council of Edinburgh. The magistrates, to encourage the citizens to purchase the oak trees growing thereon, gave them permission to new-front their houses seven feet forward with that material —a proceeding which narrowed the principal street fourteen feet. These wooden-fronted houses, or as they were named in Scotland 'Timmer Lands,' were, however, a leading feature in European architecture of the sixteenth and seventeenth centuries ; and to this characteristic many of the ancient towns in Germany and Flanders, and our own Chester in England, owe their beauty of old-world quaintness.   There was an inner stone structure of substantial masonry.   Taylor, the English Water-poet, in his *Pennylesse Pilgrimage*, describes the walls of these 'goodlie houses' as 'exceeding strong, not built for a day, a weeke, a monthe, or a yeare, but from Antiquitie to Posteritie for many Ages.' A wooden front was then superadded to these inner walls, supported by projecting beams.   With each story of height the projections increased, till in some of the closes it was possible for the occupants of opposite attics to shake hands, and hold some small convivialities with each other.   In some instances the wooden fronts were left open, and formed galleries.   As a rule, these galleries were of plain beams, owing to the hardness of the Borough Muir oak, but there were examples—notably that of a house near the corner of Blackfriars Wynd, where the rich carving of the front façade showed near relationship to the magnificent old balconies of Bruges and Ghent in the time of Charles v.   These open galleries—a feature in the High Street especially—were adorned on gala-days with tapestries and cloths of gold, and were crowded with the dignified worth of Scottish matronhood, and with the bright beauty of Old Edinburgh's youthful daughters.

DIGNIFIED MATRONHOOD AND BRIGHT BEAUTY.

Of the earlier tenants of this 'Timmer Land' in Dickson's Close nothing is known, but in 1786 it was tenanted by David Allan, termed the Scottish Hogarth from his characteristic figure-painting.

CIVILITIES IN DICKSON'S CLOSE.

Bow-head Corner House.

I.—IN SUNSHINE.

THIS house, taken down in 1878, was one of the finest of the old timber-fronted burgher dwellings in the old city, and, from its prominent situation, the best known. It had two elevations—one towards the Lawnmarket, the other towards the West Bow. The street floor only had a stone wall, the chimneys being carried up in the gables of the houses on either side. A piazza was on the ground floor towards the Bow, and the beams of the upper floors projected over it, and over each other, with a boldness which made a stranger hold his breath. Perhaps this seeming overweighting of the house is best described in the words of one of its own tenants—an old man who had been born and who had lived for more than seventy years literally under its roof, for to him belonged the small attic windows in the gable towards the Bow. 'Feared to bide up here on a windy nicht?' said he, 'no' me! The hoose was built afore Sir Isaac Newton invented

the centre o' gravity, but, depend upon it, the man that
built it kent o' something just as guid!'   The northern

'FEARED? NO' ME!'

front was the more ornate.   On its second floor there
were Doric pilasters between the windows, which last
were filled with panels of glazed lattice-work.   A
minute examination of Old Edinburgh shows that
the 'front lands' in the High Street were tenanted
by merchants and the trading community.   The
nobility, the landed gentry, and the dignitaries of
the Church prior to the Reformation, affected the
select retirement of the closes, or the more aristocratic
suburbs of the Canongate and the Cowgate.   The

shops in the High Street had all open booths entering by a piazza the same as that of the Bow-head ; and the Luckenbooths were so named because they were closed (*lucken*), a nearer approach to the shops of modern times. A little to the north-west of the Bow-head house stood the Weigh-house or ' Butter Trone,' which was demolished in 1650 by Cromwell's orders, for

BOW-HEAD CORNER HOUSE.

interfering with the ' schottis of the Castell.' It was rebuilt at the Restoration, and was removed in 1822

from the High Street to Canal Street, a street which in
its turn has been removed to make room for the North
British Railway Station.

The Bow-head house was especially a coign of vantage on the occasions of the state entry of the rulers
of Scotland into their capital.   The law of precedent,
always powerful in Court ceremonials, was to enter the
Grassmarket by the West Port, thence up the steep
zigzag of the Bow into the High Street, then to pass
slowly down between the then unbroken lines of its
towering houses to the Nether-Bow Gate, thence by the
burgh of Canongate to the royal home at Holyrood.
In some instances the Castle was visited.   This was
done by Queen Mary on her state entry on the
2d September 1561.   She entered her capital on
horseback, followed by a great retinue of French and of
Scottish nobles, having ridden from Holyrood [1] along
the Lang Gait (now Princes Street)—sweeping round the
strength of the grey Castle Rock ; and right loyally did
the old city and its rulers receive their young Queen.
At the 'Butter Trone,' hard by the Bow-head house,
and near the upper Bow Port of the first city wall, she
was presented with the keys of the city—not by the
Chief Magistrate, as is now the wont, but—by 'ane
bonny bairn,' who issued as if it had been 'ane angel'

---

[1] On this occasion Queen Mary used the first side-saddle with a
pommel ever seen in Scotland.

from a cloud with folding leaves.   To the silver keys
were added a Bible and a Psalter, bound in purple

PRESENTATION OF THE KEYS.

velvet, whereupon, an old writer quaintly remarks,
'the bairn returned to its place, and the *clud steekit.*'

Members of the Town Council, with some 'honest nychtbours,' to the number of sixteen, bore aloft a canopy of purple velvet fringed with gold over the Queen and her palfrey. Good men and true they were, who had fought the Southron in Hertford's time, and who were ever promptly 'reddy bodin for weir' to man the city wall at the 'jow of the common bell' —for 'Bauld sword in Defens' was a primary requisite in the civic rulers of those days. On that gay September day, however, they were all clad in the black velvet and the cramoisie of the old song, and, masters on their own 'caulsay,' they took their honourable place beside their Queen, to be followed by dame and noble, squire and knight; but nathless long before the brilliant throng reached Holyrood, the good city fathers, with their canopy-carrying, would be 'sair forfeuchan.' Similar ceremonies took place on the entry of James VI. in 1579, and on that of his bride, Anne of Denmark, ten years later, when the King's 'darrest spous' was propyned with jewels worth 20,000 crowns—true evidence of the royal bridegroom's remark, that 'a king with a new-married wife doesna come hame ilka day.' Up the Bow once again came King James in 1617 from his new kingdom of England, impelled by his Majesty's own 'salmonlyke instinct' to see 'our native soyle and place of our birth and breeding.' Up the Bow came Charles I. for his

Scottish coronation at Holyrood; and up the Bow, in due time, he was succeeded by Oliver Cromwell and his Ironsides, who at Marston Moor and Naseby had turned back the battle-shock of Rupert's Royalists, as the grim Bass Rock does the swell of the ocean in a north-east gale.

UP THE BOW RODE CROMWELL AND HIS IRONSIDES.

II.—IN· SHADOW.

' Lassie,' quo' he, ' their travail 's great,
 While we sit lown an' calm ;
Bring doun, bring doun the Haly Beuk,
 We 'll sing the mornin' Psalm.'

An' we sang the mornin' Psalm, until
 The tears drapt frae oor e'e,
My faither prayed for the camp of God,
 I prayed for my brethren three.

Old Song.

As the brightest sunlight has the deepest shadows,
so was it with the old Bow-head house.   As it saw
Sovereigns pass to the throne, so was it compelled to
witness sufferers, justly or unjustly, pass to the scaffold.   From the Restoration down to 1784 the place of
public execution was in the Grassmarket, and whether
the place of previous confinement had been the Tolbooth or the Castle, it behoved the ghastly procession
to pass the Bow-head house and down the Bow.   If the
sufferer was deemed of gentle blood, however, as in the
case of Morton, Argyll, Montrose, Guthrie, and others,
the ' Maiden,' or the gibbet, was erected at the ' Mercat
Croce' in the High Street.   For twenty-eight years after
the Restoration those 'passers-by who never returned'
were chiefly the Covenanters, who, desiring to worship
the God of their fathers according to their conscience,
sealed their testimony with their blood, and, to use

the ribald words of the Duke of Rothes, one of their judges, literally 'glorified God in the Grassmarket.' During the same years, in England there was Bunyan in Bedford Jail, and the Restoration revenge on the Puritans, and ships following on the track of the *Mayflower* across the Atlantic, with brave men, self-exiled, who feared God and knew no other fear—fit hands to lay the foundation-stones of the mighty Republic of the West, on which the Pilgrim Fathers had already

GLORIFIED GOD IN THE GRASSMARKET.

graven the secret of that nation's greatness—FREEDOM TO WORSHIP GOD. And away across in France, during the very same years, there were the Dragonnades, and the Revocation of the Edict of Nantes, and an old Huguenot merchant writing with his sword on his door, 'Loyal au Roy, mais ma Foy est à Moy:'—'Loyal to the King, but my religion is my own.' In the worship of a pure God it may be conceded that a subject might have differed from the faith and practice of such monarchs as Charles II. and Louis XIV., yet, in spite of posterity having vindicated the action of these men, as it has benefited by their sufferings,—*yet*, until Thomas Carlyle came, who with no unmighty sickle

shore out the tares that had choked and hidden Truth,
burning them with no gentle hand, and with no
unbitter smoke before our eyes,—YET, until he came,
there have not been wanting writers who have stigma-
tised the martyrs' religion as fanaticism, their con-
science-scruples as narrow-mindedness, and who have
appraised their buffetings, their banishment, their
tortures, and their death by a sneer.   Amongst much
of Old Edinburgh that has passed away there is no
room to regret the *genteel history-writing* of the past
centuries, and its emasculated shadow in the present
day.

The interior decorations of the Bow-head house were
good; some of the ceilings were formed in panels with
wrought mouldings and ornamentation, and at one time
one of the rooms was decorated with Edinburgh-
made Spanish leather in crimson and gold.   We quote
again our old Bow-head informant, who was an uphol-
sterer, and an authority on the technical history of his
craft.   Upholsterers or 'tapischers' were formerly also
wall-decorators.   In the seventeenth century, stamped
leather, an artistic covering for walls and furniture, was
manufactured by Bailie Brand, afterwards Sir Alexander
Brand.   Specimens of the Scottish make are getting
rare.

𝕸ajor 𝕮eir's 𝕳ouse.

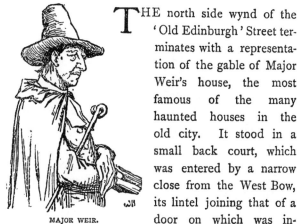

MAJOR WEIR.

THE north side wynd of the 'Old Edinburgh' Street terminates with a representation of the gable of Major Weir's house, the most famous of the many haunted houses in the old city. It stood in a small back court, which was entered by a narrow close from the West Bow, its lintel joining that of a door on which was inscribed the legend—

SOLI · DEO · HONOR · ET · GLORIA · 1604.

The narrow close was associated in the popular mind with very different work, for the story of Major Weir touches upon the witnessed palpable *personality* of Satan, and his active *bodily* interference in the concerns of men. The whole subject is surrounded with difficulties, and is now relegated to the outposts of religious belief,

c

but, in the seventeenth and eighteenth centuries, it occupied a different and a very prominent position in the minds of the Christian communities of Great Britain, and of the Puritan colonies across the Atlantic.

MAJOR WEIR'S HOUSE.

We refer the curious in these matters — and they are many — for the history of Major Weir, to a book named *Satan's Invisible World Discovered*, noting, however, that the Satan of this volume is a very different spirit from the 'archangel ruined' of Milton. This work, now little known, was once to be found on the book-shelf in the majority of religious Scottish homes : side by side with *The Pilgrim's Progress* and *The Holy War* of Bunyan, Baxter's *Saints' Rest*, Howe's *Redeemer's Tears*, and other strong food of Puritan faith, beloved by the sterner minds of our forefathers. It was written by

George Sinclair, Professor of Philosophy in the College
of Glasgow, a man of high scientific attainments, and
published at Edinburgh in 1685. Copies of the original
edition are *exceedingly rare.*

This work represents the serious side [1] of much that
was grotesque in the miracle-plays of the Romish
Church, and that has remained so in the works of many
of the early Scottish poets or 'makaris,' and notably
in the works of the national poet Burns, as seen in
'Tam o' Shanter' and the 'Address to the Deil' :—

> 'Great is thy pow'r, an' great thy fame ;
> Far kend an' noted is thy name ;
> An' tho' yon lowin' heugh 's thy hame,
>   Thou travels far ;
> An' faith ! thou 's neither lag nor lame,
>   Nor blate nor scaur.
>   .   .   .
> When twilight did my grannie summon,
> To say her pray'rs, douce, honest woman !
> Aft yont the dyke she 's heard you bummin',
>   Wi' eerie drone ;
> Or, rustlin', through the boortrees, comin',
>   Wi' heavy groan.

Annexed is a reprint of the title-page of the first
edition of *Satan's Invisible World Discovered*, which
tells its own tale.

[1] The pitiful side of the subject is seen in the following quotation
from Nicoll, 9th March 1659 : ' There were fyve wemen, witches,
brunt on the Castell Hill, all of them confessand their covenanting
with Sawtan, sum of them renunceand their baptism, and all of
them oft tymes dancing with the Devell.'

Satans Invisible

WORLD

DISCOVERED;

OR,

A choice Collection of Modern Relations, proving evidently againſt
the *Saducees* and *Atheiſts* of this
preſent Age, that there are *Devils,*
Spirits, Witches, and *Apparitions,*
from Authentick Records, Atteſta-
tions of Famous Witneſſes, and
undoubted Verity.

To all which is added,
That Marvellous Hiſtory of *Major Weir,*
and his Siſter:

With two Relations of Apparitions at
Edinburgh.

By Mr. *George Sinclar,* late Profeſſor of Philoſophy,
in the College of *Glaſgow.*

No Man ſhould be vain that he can injure the merit of
a Book, for, the meaneſt Rogue may burn a City, or
kill an Hero, whereas, he could never build the one,
or equal the other. Sr. G. McK.

Edinburgh, Printed by *John Reid.* 1685.

Major Weir was burned at the Gallowlee, between Edinburgh and Leith, in 1670, and his sister Jean, otherwise Grizell Weir, was hanged in the Grassmarket. The whole story is believed now to have been a tissue of crime and superstition, which ended in madness.

Earl of Ibynoforo's Ibouse.

THIS very picturesque building was in South Gray's Close, though its principal entrance was from the adjoining Hyndford's Close. Its style was a combination of the early Border Tower, on which were grafted the features of the Franco-Italian influence, which began to affect Edinburgh architecture after the Restoration. For many years this mansion was the residence of the Earls of Selkirk, and afterwards of the Earls of Hyndford, who latterly removed to No. 8 St. John Street. This peerage became extinct in the person of Andrew Carmichael, sixth Earl, in 1817, when the art treasures of a succession of ambassadors, from the time of James VI. onwards, were sold by public auction.

The Hyndford Close house now became the property of Dr. John Rutherford, Professor of the Practice of Medicine in the University of Edinburgh. Dr. Rutherford was a Borderer, a son of Yarrow Manse, and was educated at Selkirk. He studied at the Universities of Edinburgh, Leyden, Paris, and Rheims. At Leyden he was the pupil of Boerhaave, the most celebrated physician of the eighteenth century. Following the example of his

famous master in Holland, he was the first in this
country to institute the practice of giving clinical lec-
tures to his
students,
which he did
in the Royal
Infirmary,
1748. His
College lec-
tures were de-
livered in
Latin, as was
then the cus-
tom through-
out Europe;
but these
clinical lec-
tures were
given in the
vigorous Bor-
der vernacular

EARL OF HYNDFORD'S HOUSE.

—kindliest of Scottish dialects—and what a great
relief this must have been to many an eager young
student-mind *hirpled* by meagre scholarship !

The mother of Sir Walter Scott—Anne Rutherford—
was Dr. Rutherford's only child by his first marriage,
and her girlhood was passed in this very pleasant old

city home.   To school she went in the neighbouring
Blackfriars Wynd, taught by a worthy gentlewoman,
Mrs. Euphame or Effie Sinclair, of the ancient house

of Longformacus, who, if
judged by results as seen
in her pupils, must have
been possessed of a culti-
vated mind well stored in
literature, in addition to
the thorough housewifely
training — so pleasant a
feature in the girl-educa-
tion of the eighteenth
century.   Married in 1758
to Walter Scott, W.S.,
Anne went to her new
home, on the third flat of

TO SCHOOL SHE WENT.

the house in College Wynd, where, in 1771, her dis-
tinguished son was born, to whom she was a good,
able, loving, and much-loved mother.

The Hyndford Close house afterwards became the
property of her half-brother, Dr. Daniel Rutherford,
Professor of Botany, the King's Botanist for Scotland,
and a chemist, moreover, of European fame.

To Sir Walter Scott, when a lad at the neighbouring
High School and subsequently, this house, with its
inmates and its surroundings, was a second home.

The Nameless House.

THIS building stood in the Cowgate, in the antique row of houses between the College Wynd and the Horse Wynd, on the east side of St. Peter's Pend, and near Symson's house. It is a good specimen of picturesque street architecture attained by simple means. The effect of the double row of dormer windows and the high crow-stepped gable containing the stair is at once bold and pleasing.

The builders of these old houses understood the junction or meeting-point of roof and sky better than the architect who planned the new Edinburgh across the Nor' Loch in 1768. HOUSE FROM COWGATE. The mile-long granary-like sameness of front elevation, and the carefully ruled roof summit lines which came

41

into fashion with early Princes Street, are an example
in point—a state of matters from which that street,
perhaps the most beautifully situated in the world, has
been freeing itself with vigorous rapidity in these later
days.

There is no historical clue all down the centuries to
any inhabitant of this house. The initial letters at the
foot of the page, doubtless those of the original
owner and his spouse, were engraved on the lintel, which
to us looked somewhat like a gravestone. The name-
lessness of the house is typical of the now forgotten
units of the people who dwelt within its walls—part of
the unnoted and unnumbered population of the old city,

> ‘ Who have worked their work, and reap
> The unfathomable sleep ’

of the dead within its old churchyards.

TABLET ON COWGATE HOUSE.

Laus Deo House.

THIS house stood on the north side of the Castle Hill, at the head of Blyth's Close. It bore the legend

LAVS DEO

R · M · 1591

in finely-twisted, hand-wrought iron letters on its front. It is an open question with antiquarians whether this house formed part of the adjoining Palace of Mary of Guise, or whether it existed as an independent building. The back portion of the house bore internal evidence of being erected at the same time as the Guise Palace. The elevation of polished ashlar to the front street was of more modern erection. At the iron date given, 1591, Mary of Guise had been in her tomb at Rheims in France for thirty years, and Fotheringay had seen her daughter's sorrows ended in 1587. The original title-deeds of the building are lost. The earliest existing are two contracts of alienation, in favour of James Rynd and Robert M'Naught, merchant-burgesses, in 1590. Probably the original front had been in wood, like those of the adjoining houses, and these sensible citizens appear conjointly to have re-fronted the building with stone the next year; in token of which there was sculptured on one of the lowest crow steps a shield bearing an open hand—symbol of amity and mutual proprietorship. The initials R. M., in our opinion, do not re-present Maria Re-gina, but RYND— M‘NAUGHT.

LAUS DEO HOUSE.

In an apartment on the second story of this house, but entering from Blyth's Close, the discovery of a most exquisitely painted ceil-ing on wood was made in 1840 by Mr. Cumberland Hill, now the honoured Chaplain to St. Cuthbert's Poorhouse, and author of the *Reminiscences of Stock-bridge.* Acting on the hint of a little lad that a gold star was seen above a window soffit, he scrambled up

through a hole in an ordinary stucco ceiling that had
been constructed below. Calling in the assistance of
a friend, Wil-
liam Munro,
now long
dead, the
house was
rented for a
time, and
these young
artisan artists
made exact
and spirited
representa-
tions of the
whole ceil-
ing, and for

THOUGHT THEY WERE COINERS.

five months spent all their evening hours over their
labour of love—falling meanwhile under the amusing
suspicion of the neighbours that they were coiners!

The ceiling itself, or rather a fragment of it, was
placed in the Antiquarian Museum,[1] but not till the

A painting in oil of the centre compartment is in the Antiquarian
Museum, but the drawings were unfortunately sold at the sale of
Charles Kirkpatrick Sharpe. Prior to this, they were used by Dr.
Daniel Wilson, author of *Memorials of Edinburgh*, to illustrate
a lecture which he gave on this ceiling before the Society of Anti-
quaries of Scotland.

falling in of a chimney-stalk, in a thaw after a severe
snow-storm, had broken it, and the melted snow had
spoiled its rich colouring. The ceiling was arched, and
painted in distemper. In the centre was a large
circular compartment containing a representation of our
Saviour in royal robes as a king, the vivid blue back-
ground making the figure stand out as if living. In
gold letters on the same deep blue ground, and
encircling it, were the words—

EGO · SUM · VIA · VERITAS · ET · VITA

—I am the Way, the Truth, and the Life.

There were other frescoes, each in its separate compartment. The strangest of these was an allegory of the
Christian life, painted before John Bunyan dreamed his
dream in Bedford Jail to be 'his ministrie to all
posteritie.' In this northern *Pilgrim's Progress* Christian is seen standing on the deck of an ancient ship in
full sail, speeding swiftly over the Sea of Life; above
him are the letters V. Æ., a contraction for *Vita Æterna*
—Life Eternal. The City of Destruction is burning in
the distance; Death riding on a horse amidst the waves
is aiming an arrow at his heart. Overhead is Satan, with
black wings, marked *Diabolus*. Another great dragon
of the deep, marked *Persecutio*, is pursuing the ship,
but overhead, in the sky, is the word יהוה—the Hebrew
symbol for Jehovah,—shining with a glory as of the sun,

and a hand comes forth from the glory holding a golden
chain, which is linked to the ship. Seeing the hand
and the chain, one knows that Christian will be brought
through storm and tempest at last unto his desired
haven, even as the Christian and the Hopeful of our
childhood passed through Bunyan's River of Death—
broad, black, bridgeless,—unto the shores of the
'Delightsome Land.' The other pictures were Jacob's
Dream, the Baptism of Christ, Death on the Pale
Horse, and Jesus Asleep in the Storm. This last picture
gives the means of approximating the date of its pro-
duction. For the scenery on the shores of the Sea of
Galilee there is substituted a north view of Edinburgh—
from Salisbury Crags and Holyrood to the Castle ! This
would demonstrate that the painter was Edinburgh-born,
in his desire to place his native city as near as possible to
that most beautiful, most sacred, and now most silent of
waters. The representation of bold crags on the far side
from Tiberias is a truth, as we are able to testify from
having noted a resemblance when on the spot ; but the
sight of the steeple of the last Nether-Bow Gate, erected
1606, and that of the old Weigh-house, taken down
1650, raises a kindly smile over the pleasant conceit—
a conceit not unusual in pictures of the time. The
dates given show that the whole ceiling adornment, a
work of undoubted genius and great labour, must have
been done in the earlier half of the seventeenth century.

The first quarter of the seventeenth century was a
time of mercantile prosperity to both kingdoms. The
strife for religious liberty had not begun in Scotland,
nor that for civil liberty in England. King James's
favourite text was 'Blessed are the peacemakers,' and
under its influence he stretched out an appreciative
hand to Learning and Art, and encouraged the esta-
blishment of new manufactures in the capital of his
'auncient kingdom.'

THESE YOUNG ARTISANS MADE EXACT REPRESENTATIONS
OF THE CEILING.

The Cunzie-House.

THE Cunzie-House, or 'Cunyie Nook,' stood on the west side of the Candlemaker Row, where it joined the Grassmarket, and fronted the Cowgatehead. Its timber-arched porch, its outside stairs, and its ancient 'ballusters' gave it a picturesque individuality of appearance, which was heightened by its wooden eaves, rhones, and brackets, and by its crow-stepped gables decorated with cope pediments. Money was coined in Scotland from the time of Alexander I. till the Union in 1707. The locality of the Mint varied. Besides this Cowgatehead Cunyie Nook, which was used in the regency of Mary of Guise, there was in Edinburgh an earlier Mint, on the west side of the Abbey Close at Holyrood. Another is mentioned in the examination of Darnley's murderers as being on the south side of the Canongate, opposite the Tolbooth; but the existence of this Mint is not elsewhere mentioned. Another Cunzie-House was in the Castle. It was destroyed in the ruinous siege of 1573. Coining was not confined to the capital. Stirling, Linlithgow, Roxburgh, Dundee,

D

Dumbarton, Perth, and Aberdeen have each for a longer or shorter time possessed a Royal Scottish Cunzie-house.

In 1574 the Scottish Mint was finally established by Regent Morton in the specially erected and semi-fortified building in South Gray's Close.   The legend

BE · MERCIFVL · TO · ME · O · GOD · 1574

on the tower over its main entrance may have been the

choice of that strange two-sided nature. Here the Mint remained till the Union of the Parliaments in 1707, when the Scottish dies were all destroyed.

From it and from the other Cunzie - houses were issued the Lyon-pieces and the Uni-corns, the

THE CUNZIE-HOUSE.

Angel-pieces and the Bonnet-pieces, the Nobles and

the Nonsunts, the Ryders and the Ryals, the Merks and the Half-merks, the Crown Groats and the Groats of the Flower-de-luce, the Pennies and the Placks, the Bodles and the Bawbees—all current coin of the realm of Scotland, and whose names are enshrined to us still in its history and song.

GOLD COIN—FRANCIS AND MARY—1558,

Paul's Wark.

THIS building, which stood at the foot of Leith
Wynd, was built by the Magistrates in 1619 as
a charitable work-factory, and bore the name of St.
Paul's Wark. Prior to this there had been an
original foundation by Thomas Spens, Bishop of Aberdeen, who, for the maintenance of twelve poor men,
founded a hospital in 1479, which bore the name of
' The Hospital of Our Lady in Leith Wynd.'

In 1582 the Magistrates adjusted this foundation in
accordance with the Reformed religion, and all ' Beids-
men ' of this hospital were to be ' na Papist, but of the
trew Religion ; na Blasphemer or Swerer, Drunkard,
Cairter, Dysser, Theiffes or Pykers ; na sturdie Beggars,
bot exerceesing themselves in sum honest Trade.' The
last requirement, in the above curiously constructed
quotation, was certainly a *sine qua non*, for the whole
revenue of the Hospital under its original and its
restored foundation was only £12 sterling per annum.

In 1619 the Edinburgh magistrates entered into a
contract with William Dickson, of Delft, to bring over
four Dutch weavers to instruct poor boys and girls in
the making of woollen stuffs—' Grograms, Seys, and

Bays (baize).' It was for this purpose that this dormer-
windowed building was reconstructed. It was decorated with the Edinburgh City Arms, and over the
principal door was inscribed

GOD · BLIS · THIS · WARK · 1619.

The city, and
also private citi-
zens, subscribed
liberally to this
new work-chari-
ty; but exotic
manufactures
are too delicate
for Scottish air,
and subsidised
trade invariably
tends towards a
black balance-
sheet; conse-
quently the
undertaking col-
lapsed.

It should be
noted that Paul's Wark was a large building erected
round a green or *close*. [1] The building in the Old Edinburgh Street gives the front elevation.

PAUL'S WARK.

[1] In the English Cathedral, and also in the Old Parliament
House, acceptation of the word.

In 1632 the two eastmost houses on the south side of the close became a House of Correction, and as this was the first experiment of the reformatory idea of prison life in this country, 'ane certain Strangeir expert therein,' from England, by name William Stanfeild, was brought down to superintend its arrangement, and the east front house in Paul's Wark was allotted to him for a dwelling.   In *The Heart of Midlothian*, when Sharpitlaw is trying to elicit some story of the Porteous Mob from the faded memory of Madge Wildfire, he asks her, 'Were I to send you to the *Wark House* in Leith Wynd, and gar Jock Dalgleish lay the tawse on

JOCK DALGLEISH.

your back—' 'That wad gar me greet,' said poor Madge, 'but it wadna gar me mind.'   There appears to have been a good deal of the hangman's tawse used in St. Paul's Wark in the effort to compel 'ydill People to betake themselves to sum Vertew and Industrie.'

In 1650 the westmost house was a military hospital for General Leslie's wounded soldiers; it was afterwards a woollen manufactory, as mentioned by Arnot; and the whole edifice was eventually removed during the construction of the North British Railway.

Symson the Printer's House.

THIS timber-fronted house was on the south side of the Cowgate, near the foot of the Horse Wynd, and possibly it was one of the oldest in the district, dating from the early years of the sixteenth century. Above its massive oak door there was a fine elliptic architrave, surmounted by rich mouldings, with the inscription—

that is, *If we did as we should, we might have as we would.* We once saw a similarly rounded door architrave in oak, of the date 1515, in the same quaint lettering and spelling, but with this sage advice—

that is, *Get and save, and ye shall have.*   1515.

These proverbial and pithy mottoes were a door-ornamentation of earlier date than the religious legends, none of which in the mother tongue is older than 1543—the date when, by Act of Parliament, the Bible in the vernacular was first allowed to the people, provided always 'that no persons dispute, argue, or hold opinions of the same.' Nothing is known of the earlier inhabitants of this house, except that they must have

SYMSON THE PRINTER'S HOUSE.

belonged to the noble or the wealthy of the land.

In 1698 the upper floor was the printing-office and the dwelling-house of Andrew Symson, printer, but who, for upwards of twenty years prior to the Revolution, had been parish minister (Episcopal) of Kirkinner. Nothing is known of his early personal history; but he tells himself us that he had a University education, and was a co-disciple of Alexander, Earl of Galloway, who succeeded to the estates in 1671. Through this early friendship with the son, it is possible that Earl James was led to exercise his patronage, and give Symson the incumbency of Kirkinner about 1663. While minister of Kirkinner, he wrote the *Large Description of Gallo-way*, 1684. Symson was a man of rare Christian charity. Though his congregation dwindled down to three persons, he would give no information to the Government as to the recusant Covenanters who formed the bulk of his parishioners. In 1688, when the ecclesiastical pendulum swung to the opposite extreme of the arc, and Presbyterianism again became the established religion of Scotland, he was not one of the many curates who became Presbyterians to retain their livings, like the proverbial Vicar of Bray, who under the Tudor sovereigns changed his religion four times :—

> 'Come what will, come what may,
> I am determined to die the Vicar of Bray.'

He was 'necessitate, however, to retire to a quiet lurk-ing-place,' where he was found and cherished by the Galloway family. Long after losing his incumbency he records thankfully that 'his lot had been cast in pleasant places.'

He acted as amanuensis to Sir George Mackenzie of

Rosehaugh, the celebrated Lord Advocate, well known as the founder of the Advocates' Library in Edinburgh, and more widely notorious for his persecuting proclivities, and by the distich applied to him when dead and inside his jail-like grave in Greyfriars Churchyard—

> 'Bluidy Mackenyie, come out if ye daur !
> Lift the sneck, and draw the bar !'

In 1698 Symson edited and published a new edition of Sir George's *Observations* on the history of Statutes.

In 1705 he was the author of ' Tripatriarchicon, or the lives of Abraham, Isaac, and Jacob ;' in verse—very *hamelt*. For his rustic style he has elsewhere a versified apology, and in the Preface he gives a very quaint estimate of his own poetic merit :—' The author does not in the least expect to be classed with our famous modern English Poets. No, no ; the height of his ambition is to be ranked *inter minores Poetas ;* or, if that seems too bigg, he is content to be lifted *inter minimos:*— Providing ordinary Ballad-makers, Country Rhythmers, mercenary Epitaph-mongers, and several others of that tribe be wholly excluded the number.'

Another of his own works is a series of Elegies— thirteen in number,—now very rare. In 1706 he published his poem on the Union with England, then imminent. He was in favour of the measure. The poem is entitled ' Unio ; Politico, Poetico, Joco, Serio. A quotation is given to show a voice of ' Old Edinburgh,' from the Cowgate, on the question of a Redistribution Bill :—

> ' Thus we see
> Essex has eight (members), and Cornwall fourtie thrie ;
> London, tho' rich, wide, pop'lous, sends no more
> Than four, and little Winchelsea sends two.
> Yet London doth in everything exceed
> The others, much more than Nile doth Tweed ;
> *And yet for all these inequalities*
> *I can't see where the disadvantage lyes.'* (!)

Watson, in the Preface to his *History of Printing*, gives an account of the printing-offices of Edinburgh, and informs us that ' in 1700, Mr. Matthias Sympson, a student in Divinity, set up a small *House;* but he, designing to prosecute his Studies, left the *House* to his Father, Mr. Andrew, one of the Suffering Clergy, who kept up the *House*, till about a year ago when he died.' Watson's work was published in 1713, from which it would appear that Symson must have died early in 1712. His library was disposed of by public sale. The catalogue was printed under the title of ' Bibliotheca Symsoniana : a Catalogue of the vast Collection of Books in the Library of the late reverend and learned Mr. Andrew Symson. Edinburgh : Printed in the year 1712.' 4to. Pp. 34.

It is to be noted that on the door of this house in the 'Old Edinburgh Street' there is a *risp*, or *ringle*, or *tirling-pin*, the modest, old-fashioned precursor of door-knockers and door-bells. A risp was a twisted or serrated bar of iron standing out vertically from the door, provided with a ring, which, being drawn along the series of nicks, gave a harsh, grating sound, summoning the inmates to open. Tirling-pins are often mentioned in Scottish ballad literature, *e.g.* in 'Annie of Lochryan,' the 'Drowned Lovers,' 'Glenkindie,' and also in 'Sweet William's Ghost':—

'There came a ghost to Margaret's door
 Wi' mony a grievous groan ;
And aye he tirled at the pin,
 But answer made she none.

"Is that my father Philip ?
 Or is't my brother John ?
Or is't my true love Willie
 To Scotland now come home ? " '

Ghosts and lovers, being modest in ballads, may have tirled at the pin,—that is, touched it gently,—but it was possible for a dun seeking money to make the ring grate along the risp in a way calculated to rasp the feelings of all within the house, and hence the homely name of 'a crow,' or, in Edinburgh parlance, 'a craw,' the noise being not unlike the croak of the raven

Andrew Symson, in a small Latin vocabulary, pub

lished 1702, makes mention of this appliance by defining ' *cornix* ' as ' a crow ; a clapper or ringle.'[1]

[1] Chambers's *Traditions*, p. 226.   (Ed. 1869.)

'THERE CAME A GHOST TO MARGARET'S DOOR,
AND AYE HE TIRLED AT THE PIN.'

The Oratory of Mary of Guise.

THE Oratory of Mary of Guise stood on the east side of Blyth's Close on the Castle Hill. Its doorway was half-way down the close, opposite the chief entrance to her Palace. The whole formed an extensive range of building which stretched westward over the areas of Tod's Close and Nairn's Close, having, as was the wont in these unsettled times, various exits and entrances to all the three closes. The Guise Palace was erected after the English invasion of 1544. The Palace and Abbey of Holyrood and the whole burgh of Canongate were situated outside the city wall, —the powerful defence of 'Abbey Sanctuary' having been sufficient for protection in warfare till Hertford came, who had respect 'for neither monke nor masse, priest nor devil.' It was a divided and an unprepared Scotland that awaited him. Queen Mary was an infant of months, and the contending parties of the Regent Arran, of the Queen-Mother, and of Cardinal Beaton, were striving for pre-eminence. The instructions given by Henry VIII. to his lieutenant were vast; Hertford's performance was thorough. Arran withdrew, the Cardinal, unlike his fighting uncle, fled in terror to Stirling, and the only leader left in Edinburgh at this strait, with brains and a sword-arm, was Sir Adam Otterburn, the Provost, who, with the citizens, and amongst them Halkerston, of Halkerston's Wynd, fought 'rycht lustilie, and monie of thame to the deid,' for their city and their infant Queen. As it was the Cardinal and the extreme Church party who had foiled

MARY OF GUISE'S ORATORY.

Henry's matrimonial intentions for his son, Hertford's vengeance fell sorely upon them, and the religious houses of the Lothians and the Merse, including Holyrood Abbey and Palace; and subsequently the four rich Abbeys of the Border—Melrose, Dryburgh, Jedburgh, and Kelso,—were burned and pillaged by this marriage-thwarted iconoclast.

Holyrood being no longer safe as a royal residence, the selection of this site on the Edinburgh
Castle Hill by the Queen-Mother showed both judg-

CLEAR THE CAUSEWAY.

ment and great refinement of taste.   Safety was
guaranteed by the Palace being under the protection

of the Castle guns, and annoyance from the not uncommon street 'tuilzies' was guarded against by its
being placed behind the 'fore lands' of the Castle Hill,
and well up the close.   Closes in those days were all
provided with gates, promptly closed on the first cry of
'Clear the causeway!' The crook hinges on which
these gates hung were placed a short distance in from
the main street.   They used to be a common enough
sight to the antiquary, but they wellnigh disappeared a
few years ago when iron and batting lead were at their
highest quotations in the market,—'pykit oot,' it is said,
by small speculative fingers.   Another evidence of wise
foresight was seen in an old-fashioned draw-well *inside*
the Oratory walls; its waters ever inexhaustible,—clear
and cold in the hottest day of summer.

As regards beauty of prospect, it is very questionable
if there is a royal residence existing that can equal that
which this Guise Palace possessed to the seaward side.
Edinburgh, like Jerusalem of old, is beautiful for situation 'on the sides of the north.'   True, the immediate
foreground is now very different from the time when
Mary of Lorraine saw her gardens sloping sharply down
to the Nor' Loch, with the site of Modern Edinburgh,
then a heathy moor, lying beyond; but the everlasting
hills are the same—near at hand, the strength of the
Maiden Castle Rock; Ben Lomond, Ben Ledi, and
Ben Voirlich in the far north-west; the green Ochils,

E

and Fife, with her golden girdle of towns on which the
sunbeams love to rest; Inchkeith, the Bass, North

IS THERE A ROYAL RESIDENCE THAT CAN EQUAL ITS
BEAUTY OF PROSPECT?

Berwick Law, Arthur Seat, and the far beyond of the
sea,—a prospect truly where one realises how very far

the east is distant from the west,—and beautiful enough
and changeful enough in morning-time, at noontide,
and in evening light, in sunshine and in storm, to
satisfy the longing of mind and spirit.

The internal decorations of Palace and Chapel, taken
as a whole, were the finest of any in the Old Edinburgh
houses. The massive mantelpieces in the principal
apartments were of stone, with pillared supports, or with
grouped Gothic shafts rose-adorned.   In two of the
Oratory rooms, prior to 1820, were two carved oak
mantelpieces, the four pilasters of which had com-
posite capitals with figures of the four Evangelists
beautifully undercut.   The oak for the beams and
finishing was not the home-grown oak of the Borough
Muir, which was used for the fronts and beams of the
' Timmer Lands '—a wood hard enough perhaps for a
cannon ball to strike through without splintering, but also
fatally hard for the carver's tools.   It was a sea-borne
oak that was employed, and in all likelihood imported
for the special purpose from the Baltic—possibly from
Dantzic, with which city Scotland had an early and a
prosperous trade.   This oak was of large size, beautifully ' chamfered ' and more easily worked. It is strange
that one of these beams, when opened after having
been in its resting-place for more than three hundred
years, gave out the same forest bark odour to the saw,

and was as fresh as if it had come over the German Ocean with the wood cargo of last autumn.

Originally, the under rooms of the Oratory had as a ceiling, the beams supporting the floor above, displayed. These were ornamented on three sides with conventional designs in gold and colours. The oak carvings successively removed from the Chapel proper were very fine, and showed the high position which this art then held in Scotland. Specially noteworthy were a series of trusses with long pendant finials of pomegranates, grapes, and leaves full-size, in high relief, and boldly cut. The whole of the carving was executed with a bold freedom, combined with delicacy, which is the characteristic of old Scottish carving before the Reformation era, and the best exemplification of which are the famous Stirling Heads—the medallions which, prior to 1777, formed the ceiling of the King's Presence-chamber in Stirling Castle. In the midst of a plethora of nominally old carved oak that is spurious, and of much that is good but which is utterly apocryphal in its history, one regards these Stirling Heads—each a historical portrait —as the standard of Scottish oak carving. We inherit the opinion of the best judge of old oak that we ever knew, in saying that the same hand which carved the Stirling Heads carved the ornamental wood-work in the Guise Palace and Oratory. The artist who was employed by James v., at Stirling, 1529-39, and who

carved the characteristic medallion portraits of that
monarch, and of Mary of Guise herself, would naturally
be summoned to adorn the new Palace of her widow-
hood, built some twelve years later.[1]

A gallery on the first floor passed over the Close
from the Palace to the Oratory, and at the right hand
of the fireplace there was a niche in the richest style of
Decorated Gothic architecture. It was probably used
for the display of some of the altar-service plate.
Behind this niche was found a small iron coffer, which
is now at Abbotsford. These niches were a feature in
both the Oratory and the Palace. There were seven
in all. Only one, however, had a drain-hole, which is
the distinctive mark of a piscina of the Roman Catholic
Church. In it the officiating priest rinses the chalice
at the celebration of the Mass, and washes his hands.
Several years ago, when a piscina was removed out of a
private chapel in Barringer's Close, we were curious to
trace the course of the drain-hole, knowing that pipes
existed not in Old Edinburgh. Mounting a ladder, we
picked it out, and found it was drilled through a course
of solid stone to the front of the building : the water
then simply dropped down on the pavement below.

[1] Ten of these medallions, sold at the late Lord Cockburn's
sale in 1854, were purchased by the late Marquis of Breadalbane,
and are now in the possession of the Honourable R. Baillie
Hamilton at Langton.

When 'Gardyloo' (*gardez l'eau*) was one of the voices of the night, a shower of comparatively pure water—blessed or unblessed—would be a mere bagatelle!

In this work it is not possible to go into the detail of the Palace ornamentation and arrangements, with its panelled walls, its arched roofs, its emblematic ceiling paintings, its heraldic blazonries; its 'Deid Chalmer,' black in colour and sorrowful in its suggestiveness; its secret chamber, which, entering by a moveable panel, and issuing by a secret stair, wound round the *outside* of an ordinary turnpike, unknown and unsuspected for generations.

There is little doubt that the furnishing of the Oratory and Palace of Mary of Guise would be in keeping with the artistic beauty of the internal decoration.

It was the age of the triumphs of the goldsmith's art and kindred work—the Renaissance age of the

GARDYLOO !

Medicis in Italy, and of Francis I. and Henry II. in France.

Without speaking of the possibility of specimens of the rare gold and silver work of France, then in one of its best periods, as commissions or presents from her daughter—the Dauphiness, and subsequently the Queen, of that artistic nation during the years of the Oratory's existence as a religious building—we are safe in saying that the 'Chapel Graith' would be in keeping, and fully equal to that of the Old Edinburgh High Kirk of St. Giles at the Reformation.   The Inventories of St. Giles's Church in the Edinburgh City Records tell of the Great Eucharist, or Communion Cup, with golden 'weiks' and stones; *item*, a unicorn and a pix of gold; *item*, a silver ship for incense; *item*, altar-cloths and priestly vestments in gold brocade and in crimson velvet embroidered with gold, and a detailed profusion of church service-plate wrought in the precious metals —the mere enumeration of which makes the usually commonplace pages of an inventory read like those of a treatise on Art.   As to the Palace furniture, we read in *The Inventories of Mary Queen of Scots*, published by the Bannatyne Club, that the Queen Regent—Mary's mother—possessed 12 sets of tapestry, one of these containing the 'historie of the judgement of Salamon, the deid barne, and the twa wiffis,' the tapestry being 'maid of worsett, mixt with threid of gold;' *item*,

5 palls or cloths of state; *item*, 2 Turkey carpets—a floor-covering that has altered neither in texture nor in colour from her time to our own day. Her daughter, Queen Mary, owned 36 of these carpets, a luxurious possession of such moveables even in the present age; but then she returned to Scotland as the wealthy 'Reine Douairière'—the Regina Dotaria—of France: strange title for the girl-widow of eighteen!

In the Guise Palace and Oratory, without and within, there was a redundance of the beauty of Nature and Art, of luxury and refinement, if there had only been rest of mind to enjoy it withal.

After the resignation of the weak Regent Arran, Mary of Guise became his successor, and it was in the early years of her regency that she occupied her Castle Hill Palace.

It was no woman's hand—especially no foreign woman's hand—that could hold the reins of government in the mid career of a Scottish religious revolution. Mary was entirely under the influence of France, and under the guidance of her six brothers of the house of Guise, and, with many good qualities, she possessed the hereditary insincerity of her people, 'the brood of false Lorraine.'

The Scottish Stewarts were a straightforward race of kings; of them the old distich was true,

> ' The Kingis word
> Is cross on swurd,'—

that is, the King's word is as the oath of another man sworn on the cross-hilted swords worn by the Crusaders, and used to witness an oath as kissing the Bible is now ; and often, moreover, held up to comfort the glazing eyes of the dying warrior in battle. It was not so with the house of Guise, and from her dates that obliquity of speech, that unroyal swerving from truth, which crops out in several of her Stewart descendants. To quote the words of her grandson King James:—'I ken the story of my grandmother, the Queen-Regent, that after she was inveigled to break her promise to some mutineers at a Perth meeting, she never saw a good day, but from thence, being much beloved before, was despised by her people.' [1]

After the Queen-Regent's death, in 1560, the building for two centuries and a half passed down in the occupation of wealthy tenants, but at last it was divided into small houses.

The whole was taken down in 1845 for the erection of the Assembly Hall and College of the Free Church of Scotland.

[1] Burton, vi. 61.

The Royal Porch.

THIS gate, with its finely-groined Gothic roof, was the chief entrance from the city into the courtyard of Holyrood Palace. It was built by Robert Bellenden or Ballantyne, Abbot of Holyrood, about 1490. Father Augustine Hay records of this Abbot Bellenden, that 'he brocht hame the gret bellis, the gret brasin fownt; . . . he theikit the kirk with leid; he biggit ane brig of Leith, ane other ouir Clide, with many other gude workis.' The great brazen font, used for the royal baptisms, was stolen in the Earl of Hertford's campaign in 1544, and was presented to the Church of St. Albans by Sir Richard Lee; but 'illgotten gear does not thrive' even in a church, for it disappeared in the troublous times of Charles I. King James VI. was baptized in a font of gold, weighing 333 ounces, a gift from Queen Elizabeth, which in its turn was coined by Queen Mary into 5000 crowns, to defend her own and Bothwell's cause against the confederated nobles.

The bridge which the good Abbot Bellenden built at

Leith was the first stone bridge over the Water of Leith. It had three arches, joining South Leith to North Leith, and existed till 1788, when it was replaced by the draw-bridge at the foot of the Tolbooth Wynd. He also erected the Church of St. Ninian, which remained the parish church of North Leith till 1816.

ROYAL PORCH.

Abbot Bellenden's own house adjoined the Royal Porch, and, in 1753, both were remorselessly demolished by the Duke of Hamilton, the Hereditary Keeper of the Palace, who employed the soldiers of the regiment then garrisoned at Edinburgh to do the work.

Swan-like, the Royal Porch is made to sing its own

dirge in a poem by Claudero, entitled ' The Echo of the Royal Porch of Holyrood House, which fell under Military Execution, Anno 1753 ' :—

' They do not always deal in blood,
Nor yet in breaking human bones,
For, Quixot-like, they knock down stones.
Regardless they the mattock ply,
To root out Scots antiquity.

MARY OF GUISE.
(*From a wood carving formerly in Stirling Castle.*)

The Tolbooth.

FROM the reign of James III. down till 1817 there existed a street, once the best business thoroughfare of the city, between St. Giles's Church and the north side of the High Street. It narrowed the width of the High Street to fourteen feet, it was separated by a crooked passage from the church, it hid the fine front of that sacred edifice, and its name was The Luckenbooths. Its most easterly house, facing the Canongate, was latterly Creech's Land, with Allan Ramsay's Circulating Library on its first floor ; and at the west end of this interjection of a street—so pleasingly named—was the Tolbooth, the 'Auld Tolbuith,' the Heart of Midlothian, the *Pretorium Burgi de Edinburgi*, which in its time had been Parliament Hall, Court of Justice, Council Chambers, and which at last was degraded into being the common prison of the city of Edinburgh.

The crooked narrow lane on the High Kirk side was well known by the name of the 'Krames,' and of it Sir Walter Scott writes :—'To give some gaiety to this sombre passage, a number of little booths or shops, after

THE HIGH STREET IN THE SEVENTEENTH CENTURY.

the fashion of cobblers' stalls, were plastered, as it were, against the Gothic projections and abutments, so that it seemed as if the traders had occupied every " buttress and coigne of vantage " with nests, bearing the same proportion to the building as the martlets' did in Macbeth's castle.' The Frauenkirche at Nuremberg is be-nested in a similar manner to the present day. *Kramerei*, a good German word of extensive grasp, well describes the nature of the goods sold round both cathedrals ; and ' Krames ' are still well known to the young at Scottish country fairs—now waxing so faded and so few.

The building of the Tolbooth was condemned in Queen Mary's time (1561) as old and unsafe; but it appears to have remained on as the prison while the New Tolbooth, or the Laigh Council-House, was built, at the south-west corner of St. Giles', for the accommodation of the High Courts of the land and the Civil Council.

Howard the philanthropist visited the prison in

REFERENCE TO THE DIAGRAM.

A The City Guard-house.	GG The Krames.
B The Mercat Cross.	H The Parliament House.
C The Pillory.	I The Lawnmarket.
D The High Kirk.	J The Weigh-house.
E The Luckenbooths.	KKK The West Bow.
F The Tolbooth.	L The Cowgate.
M The Grassmarket.	

1782, and, returning in 1787, expressed regret that it had not been removed ; but the overwhelming import· ance of the foreign legislation, consequent on the wars of the French Revolution and of Napoleon, turned attention from social and domestic politics, and thirty years were added to its old age before it was taken down in 1817.

The Tolbooth was five stories high. The eastern and original portion, built of polished ashlar—in all probability as old as the Stewart dynasty—was the felons' prison. The western, a later addition built of rubble-work, of the time of Charles I., was the debtors' prison. The principal features to the south are the two turnpike stairs. Once inside the building, these wheel stairs were dark, steep, and bewildering. A slippery pendent rope from the floor above guided the stranger, and in the darkness he was invariably informed that it had been used for hanging some criminal !

At the extreme west end there was a projection, two stories high, the flat roof of which served as a plat-form for executions, the gallows being projected from a hole in the west gable above. The last sentence of the law was carried out here from 1785 to 1817, when the place of execution was changed to the head of Libber-ton's Wynd.

Sketches of the northern elevation to the High Street are rare. In fact, so narrow was the main thoroughfare at this place that a view of the north side of the Tolbooth could only be got by craning the neck and straining the eyes upward; but the architectural beauty of the windows in the old section bore witness, in the degradation of its later days, of the time when it was the Parliament Hall and the Court House of the kingdom. Above these windows, on the summit of its pointed gable, was the topmost iron pin of the Tolbooth —a pinnacle of degradation reserved for the blood stained heads of the greatest State criminals.

In 1581 the head of the Regent Morton was placed here, 'sett up on a prick on the highest stone of the gabell of the Talbuith, toward the publict street.' Here, in 1650, was placed the head of Montrose from the gibbet, to be suc-ceeded, in 1661, by that of the Marquis of Argyll from the 'Maiden,'—'both by merit raised to that bad eminence;' for, apart from all the virtues and all the crimes alternately attri-buted to either statesman by successive generations  of love and hate, there is no doubt that both these great men, seeing what they thought RIGHT so differently,

F

fell victims to party vengeance, consequent upon a change of government.

In this matter let it be conceded that the present has improved upon the past. A change of Her Majesty's

Ministry does not send a flight of its predecessors away into the nearest enemy's country ; neither does a Prime Minister nor the eader of the Opposition grimly regard his opponent's head as a fit and possible ornament to be *spiked* on the front elevation of our civic buildings.

Below the decorated windows of this gable the street had the name of ' The Puir Folks' Purses,' from its being the place where the

A BEDESMAN.

Bedesmen, or King's Blue Gowns,[1] got their yearly dole. On Maundy Thursday,[2] or, as it was termed in

----

[1] *E.g.* Edie Ochiltree.
[2] The *Cœna Domini* of the Romish Church.

Scotland, *Skyris Furisday*—the Thursday before Good
Friday—it was the custom for Royalty, following that
of the Pope, to wash the feet of sundry poor people,
on whom blue gowns[1] and money were afterwards
bestowed. In 1585, James VI. altered the King's
Maundy to his own birthday (in June), and gave
'nyneteen gownis of Blue Claith, nyneteen purses, and
in ilk purse nyneteen schillingis, to nyneteen aiget men,
according to the yeiris of his Hienes' age.'

The opening of this purse was a puzzle to the un-
initiated, and each Bedesman wore a round leaden
badge inscribed with the words—PASS AND REPASS.
The 'Blue-goun Dole' was the earliest morning act in
the vigorous celebration of the King's Birthday in Old
Edinburgh, as sung by Fergusson :—

> ' Sing likewise, Muse, how Blue-goun bodies,
> Like scare-craws new ta'en doun frae woodies,
> Come here to cast their clouted duddies
>   An' get their pay ;
> Than them what magistrate mair proud is
>   On King's birthday ? '

The Blue Gowns had to hear a sermon ; the audience
failed in restful attention. It was preached early in
the morning, before breakfast, and they were expected

---

[1] The blue gown was intended to be a token of our Saviour's
seamless garment.

to pray for His Majesty's long life.   The breakfast consisted of bread and strong ale, a barrel of which stood
on a gantrees at the church door.   The scene and the
crowd may be imagined—fit subject for the pencil of
a Sir David Wilkie.   In 1817 the giving of the dole
was changed to the aisle of the Canongate Church.
The custom is now extinct,[1] and it is said that on the
last occasion, instead of the *many* bagpipes, each play-
ing its own blithe lilt, there was only one pibroch
wailing the Lament, 'We return no more.'

In the matter of debtor and creditor, the old mercantile laws of Scotland, like those of Holland, were very
stringent.   By Act of the Court of Session, bankrupts
or *dyvours* had to sit on a special 'pillory of heun stane
beside the Mercat Croce,' from ten o'clock in the morning till one hour after dinner on market-days, clad in
parti-coloured garments.   In both countries the default-
ing colour was yellow.   If, however, the *dyvour* paid up
his debts in full—a not uncommon event in the old
city—he could return to his own taste in the matter
of apparel.

The street-floor of the Tolbooth was let as shops,
the roofs being of strong arched masonry.   The larger
of the two shops on the north side in the Luckenbooths
was at one time tenanted by Messrs. Inglis and Horner,
silk merchants, the latter of whom was the father of

------

[1] The last Bedesman died in 1863.

Francis Horner, M.P., one of the founders of the *Edinburgh Review*. In robbing this shop, Deacon Brodie carried away velvets and silks to the amount of £400 sterling. The goods were sent to Sheffield and sold.

In the Common Hall was a board, on which were written the following vigorous lines :—

> A prison is a house of care,
>   A place where r one may thrive,
> A touchstone true to try a friend,
>   A grave for men alive.
>
> Sometimes a place of right,
>   Sometimes a place of wrong,
> Sometimes a place for jades and thieves,
>   And honest men among.'

The governor of the prison was known as the ' Guidman of the Tolbuith ; ' and the principal entrance, and the only one latterly used, was by the carved Gothic doorway of the eastern turnpike.

The Tolbooth is accredited with one especial failing : the iron Heart of Midlothian softened to the power of Scottish clannishness, and its hand ' tint its iron grip' on criminals whose friends outside had influence, money, or brains. The former qualities were exemplified in the escape (1766) of Katharine Nairne,—a well-known but not a pleasant story ; the last by the escape (1783) of James Hay, a lad of eighteen, who, under the

Draconian laws of the age, had been sentenced to death for robbery.

The night before the execution, his father—a keeper of 'Carriers' Quarters' in the Grassmarket—by dint of

FOLLOWING THE TOPER DOWN-STAIRS.

liquor to the jailer, and sending the man out for more, aided by the calm audacity of the lad following the mellow toper downstairs on his errand, managed the escape by the very skin of the teeth. The upper iron gate, left unlocked, was passed in safety, but the great oak door closed before the young face. From the opened south window the father cried, 'Turn your hand,' the perpetual *ower-word* for the opening of the Tolbooth gate. The

under turnkey, half asleep, on the outside pavement, mechanically obeyed; and the lad—the terror of death

giving speed to his feet — fled down Beth's Wynd,
cleared the churchyard wall of the Greyfriars, and found
refuge in the ghost-haunted tomb of the 'Bluidie
Mackenzie.'

James Hay was
an 'auld callant' of
Heriot's Hospital,
whose boundary walls
adjoined the perse-
cutor's grave.

The boys of that
Institution—as is not
unusual—were some-
times in opposition to
the law and govern-
ment of the day; as
witness, in 1685, their
hanging the Hospital
watch-dog for not
swallowing the Test
Oath, which he, as
a dog holding public
office, was bound to
do. The paper on

AT BLUIDIE MACKENZIE'S TOMB.

which the Oath was written was well buttered; but
the dog licked off the butter, and spat out the paper,
which, being called an explication of the Test in imita-

tion of Argyll, they tried the poor beast by jury, found
him guilty of high treason, and hanged him—for which
satire on the Government of the day the Herioters got
into sore trouble. Their successors of 1783 were true,
however, to the honour and to the traditional clannishness of George Heriot, their founder.

Their characterless comrade had thrown himself on
their protection, and in despite of the fears of the
powers that be, with the offered reward of twenty guineas,
and in defiance of the powers of darkness, they saved
their food, clambered down the wall by night, and
managed to give him succour and sustenance till the
search grew cold.   James Hay left the Grassmarket
driving one of the Glasgow carriers' carts.   He escaped
to America, and prospered.

The central event in the history of the Tolbooth is
the Porteous Mob.   It took place in 1736—thirty-five
years before its historian, Sir Walter Scott, was born,
—and its origin, its details, and its possibilities are
still the mystery of Edinburgh.

In the yards of the High School it was a favourite
story long before Sir Walter wove it into the beautiful
web of truth threaded with fiction, which has almost
canonised the memory of the old city prison, and has
turned thitherwards the feet of literary pilgrims from
all lands.

In one of the years prior to that of the False Alarm

(1804), when Lords and Commoners occupied seats on
the same High School benches, and, like their elders,
were all fired with martial zeal, as described in *The
Antiquary*, a lithe, *yauld*, country-dressed lad joined Dr.
Adam's class. He was understood to walk some miles
every day into town by the old Gilmerton Road. He
was soon asked what rank in military or naval service
he would prefer—there being in the class generals,
colonels, captains, commodores, etc. 'Are there ony
privates?' was the cautious Scottish question, by way of
answer. 'No,' was the reply. It seems that *that* important part of the British Army had been entirely forgotten. 'Then,' said he, 'I will be a private, for *they* get
the feck o' the fechtin, and that suits me.' This answer
was admired in the 'Yairds.' It admitted him to a
degree of favour which an incomer into the Rector's
class seldom received.

Shortly after, in talking of the Porteous Mob, a
'Lordie,' otherwise 'The Brigadier,' made the claim—
a claim very frequently advanced, and generally admitted
—that the chief actors in the mob had belonged to the
nobility, grounding it on the fact that a guinea had
been left on the counter of Luckie Jeffrey's shop in
the Bow for the coil of rope taken to hang Porteous—
which munificence he held to be the action of a lord!

' It was naething but the action o' a fule to gang
and gie a guinea for what was only worth a shillin', and

plenty to pay for hanging the like o' him wi',' said the Private; 'but div ye mean to say that there are no' a hunder ordinar' Scotsmen that wud hae putten doon a guinea if their blude was up?'

'Where are they?' the Brigadier asked.

'Oh, plenty,' was the answer; 'Sir Wullie[1] up at the Parliament Close for ane; *he* could lay doon guineas an' "Sir Wullies"[2] wi' a' the lords in Scotland!'

'But he's a Sir—a Baronet,' objected 'The Bugler,' who finished off the sentence, as well as every sentence he ever uttered out of school, with one of the Castle bugle-calls.

'Yes,' said the Private, getting warm, 'but he was born a plain Wullie like mysel', and a Sir is a commoner, though he got the title sune eneugh, only he made every penny o' his siller himsel', and—'

'*I* say'—broke in the Brigadier—'*I* say that the Porteous Mob leaders were a' lords, and they had generals among them—everybody says sae,—and that nane but trained men could hae dune what they did, and—'

'*I* say they were plain Wullies, jist like Wilson himsel',' retorted the Private.

'I 'll fecht ye for 't,' said the Brigadier.

[1] Sir William Forbes, banker in Edinburgh.
[2] A familiar name for a bank-note at the end of last century.

'Dune!' replied the Private,—'the Yairds, after the schule's oot.'

'Dune!' said the Brigadier.

The fight began. The masters passed out, and saw what was going on as if they saw it not. They never interfered after school-hours, and—shades of Hector and Achilles!—were not personal combats classic?

We cannot describe that 'fecht' as it was enthusiastically recounted to us by an 'Auld High Schule Callant' more than half a century after the event. Perhaps the handling was not scientific; but 'there was nae hittin' below the belt,' as our informant proudly asserted. The combatants were fairly matched in height and weight. The Brigadier was the better boxer of the two, but the Private had the advantage in wrestling, and, whenever it came to ' close grips,' down went the Brigadier. After each round there was but a moment as breathing-time, and then—at it again. Speechless, the onlookers scarce drew breath. Something of fear was just creeping into the silence, when, in a moment, after a sudden whirl one way, and a double turn another, the Private suddenly quitted his hold, and the Brigadier fell with a thud to the ground.

Stunned for an instant, but only for *one* instant, the Brigadier got up.

'I'm no' hurt,' he said (which he was); 'but I gie in. They were a' plain Wullies and Sir Wullies, and a'

Wilsons too, and they were a' willin' to gie a guinea ;
—but O man, man, yon was an awfu' " Portsburgh
Kiss "! '

By this outburst, not common to Scottish nature, and,
in fact, entirely foreign to it, he saved himself the
intense ignominy of being *asked* to ' Gie in or spit.'
The Private, who was the more breathless of the two,
and who fought from the pure love of fighting, was not
slow in following suit.

' It was nae "Portsburgh Kiss,"' said he; ' that's where
ye gaed wrang; it was a " Liddisdale Leg;" and noo,
man, I 'll be as free as you to say that there *were* lords
at the Porteous ploy—freends o' the auld King ower the

AFTER THE FECHT.

water. My grandmother
says sae, and she was
there ; though what she
will say to twa black een
is another story.   So
we 're baith richt, and
naebody 's wrang ; and
O man, after a', hasna
this been a guid, solid,
comfortable fecht ? '

The details of the
Porteous Mob as given
in *The Heart of Midlothian* are true to the letter of
history, and true also to its historian's feelings as a

son—surely one of the best beloved—of 'Old Edinburgh.'

John Porteous, Captain of the City Guard, had been condemned to death for firing wantonly on the citizens at the execution of Wilson. A respite arrived from London, and on the morning of the 8th September 1736 the execution was stayed. That same night was the night of the Porteous Mob. The city gates were seized in detail and garrisoned, the Town Guard was surprised and disarmed, the drums broken, the Lochaber axes divided amongst the assailants; all communication with the troops in the Canongate and with those in the Castle was stopped. There was a cordon placed on the streets; people were turned back the road they came. Lord Haddington and the future statesman Lord Mansfield, rightly or wrongly, have been named as amongst the leaders. One lady was handed back to her sedan-chair, apparently by a 'baxter lad;' but she was left at her own house with a bow, which, she averred, had never been learned at an oven's mouth.

The crowd surges through the street. It is a strange mob—a riot without rioting. There is no rabble; property is untouched; life is unharmed. The Tolbooth door, battered and hammered in vain, yields to fire. Porteous is dragged out to his death—not to instant assassination, but away round the Bowhead, and down the Bow, the avengers of blood carry

him.   Just past the first bend of the steep old street his
slipper falls off.   Strange Scottish mob!   The whole

THE TOLBOOTH DOOR YIELDED TO FIRE.

people stand still till it is lifted and put on.   Again they
move on in fixed singleness of purpose.   The Grassmarket, the wonted Golgotha of execution, is reached.
The gibbet, a dyer's pole, is found ; the rope is fixed.
The struggling wretch is drawn high up into the darkness, far above the fierce Rembrandt glare of the

torches; and the act of the people's vengeance and of the people's justice is ended.

It is not of the death of Porteous that the country is proud. There may be doubt or condemnation as to the unlawfulness of the deed. The pride is in the SEQUEL. The act is a unit in History. It can never be repeated. The sequel, as in the bribe-despising fidelity to Prince Charlie, showed a one-heartedness in the nation which has never been equalled.

It was a strange mob that Edinburgh mob!—the fiercest in Europe, it is said, but surely the most faithful. Hundreds of people must have seen other hundreds; but no victim, no scapegoat, could be found, though the search was keen and the bribes were high. There was no traitor in the land; no informer in 'Old Edinburgh.' Once again it was Scottish men for Scotland, shoulder to shoulder; and the nation stood as invulnerable as the phalanx of Macedon, and as silent as the stone-lipped Sphinx that has guarded the centuries of the Nile.

The Tolbooth was taken down in 1817, and not too soon; for, whatever it may be now in the region of history and romance, its condition as a prison in the matters of sanitation and cleanliness, as described by Arnot, was a disgrace to a Christian country. There was no water-pipe, no drain-pipe, in the place; and the 'jail smell' of the Tolbooth was overpowering and proverbial.   The historian Arnot writes that he *fortified* himself to encounter it.

A fast young spark (the *genus* existed in 'Old Edinburgh'), having made a hit at the Leith Races, gave a

SMELL

fish-supper at Newhaven.   He expressed himself in the severe condemnatory style which was the fashion of young bloods, say—not a century ago—as to the smell of the village.

'In short,' said Meggie Ramsay, 'he held his nose, and *dawmed* like a lord!'

This was too much for Meg.

Deil scrape the partan face o' ye !' said she. 'The last time I saw ye was in the Auld To'buith for debt, mair be token ye're awin' me saxpence for the brod o' oysters that ye got the water caddie to wile oot o' me,—for which saxpence I 'll be obleeged to ye this meenit.   Smell !' she echoed; '*ye'll* dawm a guid honest stink where there 's nane !   The warst smell in a' Newheeven should be Paradeese to your nose after YON !   In fac', the To'buith is whiles like to gar *me* fent !'

The result of this eloquence of speech was— collapse, or, as Meggie characteristically expressed it : 'It was jist like jabbing the wind oot o' the Sabbath-day haggis wi' a darnin'-needle. Eh! ma bonnie lairdie, but it did tak' the wind oot o' his sails. Smell! he wasna blate. Smell!'

Meggie had been one of the beauties of Newhaven in her day, and her usual evening beat was in the Lawnmarket and the Castle Hill. She had a recognised 'stance' at the head of Lady Stair's Close, her friend the caddie being bound to remove the oyster shells for some small payment in kind. Amongst her customers towards the end of last century was the King's printer, Smellie, with whom were interchanged many a joke and *snell* repartee; and every Saturday evening in the season she took oysters to Principal Baird, who lived in Allan Ramsay's House in Ramsay Gardens,—it being a bargain that she was to cry 'Caller ou' in her best manner when on the terrace, so that the good Principal might hear its beautiful echo come back from the Castle rocks.

SMELL! HE WASNA' BLATE.

Any picture of Old Edinburgh would be incomplete without noting the presence

G

of the city's near and neighbourly visitors—the yellow
sand carts of Gilmerton, the butter and *soor* milk carts
of the three Calders, the *buirdly*, braw skippers of
Leith, and the gallant bearing of the comely fishwives
of Newhaven.

> ' O the herrin' likes the merry moonlicht,
>   The mackerel likes the wind ;
> But the oyster likes the dredgin' sang,
>   For it comes o' a gentle kind.'

It may also be noted here that Leith Races gave to Old
Edinburgh its yearly holiday, in much the same way as
Glasgow Fair still gives its breathing-time to labour in
the sister Metropolis of the West. The Races were
held on Leith Sands.   It was considered both correct
and fashionable for the pleasure-seekers in Auld
Reekie ' to gang doon wi' the Purse '—that is, the City's
Purse of Fifty Guineas, in a bag decked with ribbons
of all colours, was mounted on a Lochaber axe carried aloft by the chief city officer, who was attended
by the Town Guard, marching in dignified procession
to the marked time of the Auld Scottish March.
The shows, the merry-go-rounds, the krames, and the
drinking-tents were all centres of mirth ; but the last
day degenerated into a saturnalia of all-round fighting.   In 1816 the Races, the City's Purse, and the
King's Hundred Guineas were transferred to Musselburgh Links ; at which time there was an exchange of

compliments—both formal and cordial—betwixt the City Rulers and the Magistrates of the good town of Musselburgh.

On the destruction of the Tolbooth in 1817, its eastern turnpike door, successor to that destroyed by the Porteous Mob, was given to Sir Walter Scott. It was removed to Abbotsford, which about that time was going through one of its building meta-morphoses. As was natural, it was visited by neigh-bours, who seemed doubtful as to building such a piece of history into a house. This was too much for Sir Walter's faithful servant, Tom Purdie, who shared in the dubiety, though he resented the head-shaking of other people.

'Shirra,'[1] he said, 'if ye will tak my advice, ye will jist pit that door where it will be an ootside yett to nae place in parteeklar. Ane micht regret it very sair if onything bad was to happen to ony o' oor bairns. It micht dae for a stable-door if Peter[2] could be got to let it ahint his horses! Ye see, Shirra, ye maun e'en do as I say, for ane's no' free to like that iron-cloured, un-chancey, ill-deidy thing comin' aboot oor toun; it has *been grippit ower often by the hangman.*'[3]

[1] Sir Walter was then Sheriff-Substitute of Selkirkshire. It was Sir Walter's usual appellation in the country until he became Sir Walter. It was as ' Shirra' that he and Tom first *forgathered.*

[2] Peter Matthieson, the Abbotsford coachman.

[3] The above story is taken from a collection of reminiscences of

Whether the destination of the door had been already
fixed, or whether Tom Purdie's speech awakened in Sir
Walter that superstition which is latent in the finest
minds, simply because they *are* the finest—as witness
Shakespeare, more especially in his 'Sonnets'—cannot
now be said ; but the door was veritably made an 'ootside yett to nae place in parteeklar,' being hung in a
wall at the top of a stair which leads from the upper
grounds down to the kitchen courtyard—all warranted
ootside.

Here for nearly fifty years has the old door swung
which in 'Old Edinburgh' was the 'ingait and the out-
gait' of so much sin and sorrow and suffering, its iron-
nailed oak bleached by the sunshine and by the snow-
storms of Tweedside, which must surely have brought
to it no small measure of purification.

Sir Walter Scott and the Abbotsford district, dating back to the
time when Abbotsford was Cairtleyhole farmhouse.   Its dictation
gave a winter's pleasure to a near relative, who was born on ground
which marched with Abbotsford.   From the death of Sir Walter
Scott, 1832, till 1868, the greater part of the Abbotsford land
was farmed by her relatives and ours, and it was our good fortune to pass all our holidays in the old farmhouse of Kaeside,
which Sir Walter Scott had made so pleasant for his factor and
friend, William Laidlaw.   From Sir Adam Ferguson down to
Swanston and Peter Matthieson, we saw the fading out of the
Abbotsford circle and surroundings.   There is a new Kaeside, but
to many it seems that the old times were better, and certainly
more beautiful, than the new.

Robert Gourlay's House.

ON the site of the present pavement of Melbourne Place formerly stood the Old Bank Close, named in earlier days Mauchan's Close, and also Hope's Close. Here, on the ruins of the town house and the chapel which belonged to the Abbots of Cambuskenneth, and utilising the carved stones of the same, Robert Gourlay built his house, one of the most massive in the old city. It is to be noted that these stones of the earlier formation, discovered when the close was swept away, had their Popish carvings turned inward. Outside they were decorously squared. Ostensibly Robert Gourlay was a messenger-at-arms in connection with the Abbey of Holyrood, with a salary of £40 a year, and perquisites. Apart from this humble office he must have been a man of wealth and position, for, though notoriously benefiting by the favour of his royal patron James VI. in after years, he was yet wealthy enough to build this house in 1569, when James was barely three years of age.

From a remark in Calderwood's *History* one may infer that Gourlay's wealth was the result of bold mercantile

speculation, and that he profited by his lowlier duties
so near the fountain-head of authority to know when to

ROBERT GOURLAY'S HOUSE.

operate. Calderwood's statement is that on May 28th,
1574, Robert Gourlay, an elder of the kirk of Edinburgh,
was 'ordeanned to mak his publict repentance in the
kirk for the sin of *transporting wheate out of the countrie
during a dearth.*' Regent Morton, however, from whom
he had purchased this wheat-selling monopoly, screened
him from the repentance-stool, though eventually he
had to give in to the powers of the Church. Doubtless

a serviceable man to his superiors, but not beloved by his neighbours, was this Robert Gourlay. In those days of crowded, but cosy and neighbourly sociality, he desires to dwell apart, and a right-of-way case—always a dainty morsel in Scottish law—was summarily ended by King James interposing his divine right to possess the *solum* of a close ! ' Na personnis,' said the King, 'can justlie plead ony richt or entrie to ye said vennel, q^{lk} be all lawis inviolable observit in tymes bygane has pertainit, and aucht to pertene, to *us*.' His Majesty ends by a mandate to build a dyke across the close. This dyke eventually took the form of a house for Gourlay's son John. It was erected in 1588. This second house became the Bank of Scotland in 1700. The Bank, established in 1695, had occupied as its first premises a flat in one of the twelve-storied tenements in the Parliament Close, but was burned out in the Great Fire of 1700. It continued to transact all its business in this narrow *cul-de-sac* till the present building at the head of the Mound was erected in 1805. ' The Auld Bank' had on its north front the device of several stalks of wheat growing out of bones—a mediæval emblem of the resurrection,—with the motto ' SPES ALTERA VITÆ.'

Robert Gourlay's own house was built for the requirements of an unsettled age. Substantial flights of stairs led from the same point to different parts of the mansion, and it was easily convertible into several distinct residences. On its demolition in 1834, a secret chamber was discovered between the ceiling of the first story and the floor of the second. Robert Gourlay seems to have put his house at the service of the Government—doubtless for 'a consideration;' in fact, he seems to have been a man given to considerations,—and during his lifetime it had the bad pre-eminence of being a condemned cell for state prisoners of gentle blood. The turret, which is a noteworthy feature in the original building, contained a curious spiral stair, which led to the room thus used at the top of the house, and a small closet adjoining was the sleeping-place of the *lockman* in attendance. Amongst others, Sir William Kirkcaldy of Grange, his brother Sir James, and the Regent Morton, all passed over its threshold to die. One does not augur well of this Robert Gourlay, who could thus draw the shadow of the scaffold over his hearthstone. Even his piety has much of being only a wooden afterthought. The legend

O · LORD · IN · THE · IS · AL · MY · TRAIST

was sculptured over his door, but the first two words 'O LORD' were on the near side, and off the lintel, and were found to have been cut in oak and afterwards let neatly into the stone. Notwithstanding the wooden eke, Old Edinburgh wit, *snell* as its own east wind, would not be slow to grasp the dubiety of meaning, and to insinuate that Gourlay's 'traist' in princes was certainly not that of the Psalmist.

King James himself was a whilom tenant of the mansion when disturbed by the fear of Francis Lord Bothwell, or by the pangs of an impoverished exchequer, and doubtless he would find the Gourlay self-contained close a *canny bield* and a *lown*. Here also was lodged Sir William Drury, after whom Drury Lane in London was named, the commander of the English auxiliaries in the siege of Edinburgh Castle in 1573, an account of which is given by Holinshed in the first edition of his *Chronicles*, published 1577, accompanied by a map and ground-plan of the Old Edinburgh of that date.

Gourlay's grandson David retired to Prestonpans, and sold the house to Sir Thomas Hope of Craighall. Amongst its more famed after tenants was Sir George Lockhart of Carnwath, Lord President of the College of Justice, who was assassinated at the head of the close by Chiesly of Dalry. Tradition, rightly or wrongly, names the apartment in the Gourlay turret stair as the scene of 'The Last Sleep of Argyll.' The story is well known from the national fresco by E. M. Ward, R.A., in the lobby of the House of Commons at Westminster. The Earl of Argyll, son of the Marquis who suffered death under Charles II., was doomed to die by James VII. A few hours before his execution a mem-

ber of the Privy Council—one of his judges—opened
the prison door, and saw 'the great Argyll' sleeping
peacefully. 'The heart of the renegade smote him,'
says Macaulay, 'and in an agony of remorse and shame
he rushed from the place, and cried, " I have been in
Argyll's prison ; I have seen him within an hour of
eternity sleeping as sweetly as ever man did, but as for
me—" '

Sixty years after, the sorest condemnation of this act,
by the person it interested most, was written by Prince
Charles Stewart to his father—the son and heir of the
same King James VII.   The letter is dated Perth, September 10th, 1745.   It is quoted from a book entitled
The Lyon in Mourning,[1] a narrative of the Rebellion of
1745, from the Stewart point of view, written by the
worthy Bishop Forbes.   'There is one man,' writes
Prince Charles, 'whom I could wish to have my friend,
and that is the Duke of Argyll, who, I find, is in great
credit amongst them on account of his great abilities
and quality, and has many dependants by his large
fortune ; but I am told I can hardly flatter myself with
the hopes of it.   The hard usage which his family has
received from ours has sunk deep into his mind.   *What
have those Princes to answer for, who, by their cruelties,
have raised enemies, not only to themselves, but to their
innocent children !*'

---

[1] Edited under the title of *Jacobite Memoirs* of the Rebellion
of 1745, by Robert Chambers.   1834.

There is something in the leader of a forlorn hope
that goes very near to the human heart after all hope is
gone. So is it now with Scotland and her 'Prince
Charlie.' His bravery, his gallant bearing—surely that
of the older and better Scottish Stewarts,—his misfortunes, his broken life, have made him dear to the
Scottish people of every sect and persuasion. Jacobitism is no more a moving principle. It exists only as a
wistful and poetical sentiment, and Prince Charlie's
gallant venture for the crown is the one ray of light
that redeems the Restoration Stewarts from execration.
His little army was practically an army in an enemy's
country—even in Edinburgh, the capital of his forefathers. The Castle held for the Government. The
direct road to England by the Borders was guarded by
the Chief of Buccleuch—powerful, but silent—whose
grandfather had been another of the victims of
James VII. The old Duchess—Monmouth's Duchess
—the Duchess of the 'Last Minstrel'—had been dead
but thirteen years, believing to the last, moreover, in
Monmouth's prior claim to the throne. Prince Charles
and his army passed to Carlisle down through the
districts desolated by the old Covenanting persecutions.
There was no rising; the people fled. No welcome in
the north of England: Derwentwater was asleep in
his bloody grave beneath 'Hexham's holy towers,'
and the 'ever loyal North' seemed sleeping and as
silent as he;—on to the halt at Derby,—the retreat,—

the meteor victory at Falkirk, and the last sad defeat at Culloden. It was too late. Prince Charles, as he writes with his own hand, suffered for the sins of his fathers. In the Edinburgh Convention of 1689 there had been a sore strain between the blind feudal vassalage due to the old dynasty of kings and the nation's sense of violated rights. The King had fled ; the straining bonds snapped. The throne was declared FOR-FAULTED and LEFT VACANT. The 'Mene, Mene, Tekel, Upharsin' had been written against the Stewart race, and the Scottish people *as a nation* said— Amen !

IT WAS TOO LATE.

Cardinal Beaton's House.

THIS house formed the right angle of the north side of the Cowgate by its junction with the east corner of Blackfriars Wynd. In 1230, Alexander II. founded the Blackfriars Monastery on the ground afterwards occupied by the site of the old High School, and gifted the Dominican brotherhood with the Wynd that has so long borne their name. From this time down to the Revolution in 1688, when Scotland as a nation ceased to possess a hierarchy, this district remained the residence of Church dignitaries and the centre of clerical influence. This mansion was built by James Beaton, Archbishop of Glasgow, 1508-24, and afterwards Archbishop of St. Andrews—a statesman of mark in his day, but whose career is overshadowed by that of his nephew, Cardinal David Beaton, who succeeded his uncle in the Primateship, was the statesman who marred the life of James v., and who will never be forgotten in Scotland as the early persecutor of the Protestant faith.

The building was one that could easily be put into a

state of defence. The entrance was from Blackfriars
Wynd by an arched passage; thence a flight of broad steps

CARDINAL BEATON'S HOUSE.

led to the first floor,
on which were the
principal rooms.
The under flat was
arched over with
solid masonry, and
when the house was
taken down in 1874
it was found that the
space between the
arches and the floor
above was packed
with a close thick-
ness of quarry sand,
which, with the ab-
sence of wood in the
erection, would go
far to make the street
floor almost fire-
proof. The gardens
in the Beaton time
extended over the ground afterwards covered by the
Mint buildings.

The most prominent or 'kenspeckle' feature in the
house was the hexagonal tower, which, springing from a
shaft, projected at the corner of the street.

It was here, in 1520, that Gawin Douglas, poet-Bishop of Dunkeld, visited Archbishop Beaton on an errand of peace—to hinder a city combat between the Douglases of Angus and the Hamiltons of Arran. The fighting Archbishop, on the Arran side, had already donned a coat of mail beneath his lace rochet, and, though preparing for the battle, struck his breast, and swore upon his conscience that he knew nothing of the matter. 'Your conscience clatters, my Lord,' was the answer of the good Gawin, who, seeing further interference to be

THROUGH THE NOR LOCH FOR THEIR LIVES.

useless, withdrew to bear the tidings to his nephew Angus, and to pray.

The battle, known as 'Cleanse the Causeway,' and

fought upon the High Street of the capital, ended in
favour of the Douglases; and the Earl of Arran and his
son, seizing a coal-horse, threw themselves both on it,
and rode through the Nor' Loch for their lives. The
mailed Archbishop fled for refuge to the altar of the
Blackfriars, had his rochet torn from his back, and
would have been slain had not his visitor of the morning
hurried to the spot and rescued him.

> ' O Dowglas, Dowglas,
>   Tendir and trew,'

and yet to die in poverty and an exile ! [1]

In 1528, James v. resided some days in this house as
the guest of the Archbishop, and the family of Douglas
was disgraced and put to the horn. That same year
the Cardinal was made Lord Privy Seal. He arranged
the King's first marriage, with the Princess Magdalen of
France, who, when she stepped on Scottish earth, knelt
and kissed the ground for the love she bore her
husband and her husband's country ; but in forty days
she died. He then arranged the King's second marriage,
with Mary of Guise, widow of the Duke de Longueville,
and while on this mission obtained the Papal Bull that
gave St. Mary's College to the town of St. Andrews. He
was the King's adviser in the institution of the College

---

[1] This estimate of the noble family of Douglas by Sir Richard
Holland in *The Howlate* is certainly as much justified by the life
of the gentle poet Gawin as by that of the good Sir James.

of Justice in Scotland, which may be said to have in-
fefted Edinburgh anew as the capital of the kingdom;
but in the interests of France and of his Church, he
thwarted all peace with England, hindered James from
meeting his uncle Henry VIII. at York, where by tryst
he had come to meet him, and he urged on the un-
fortunate struggle which ended in the King's death from
shame and a broken heart.   His private life was openly
the heaviest scandal against his own Order, then suffering
from the pungent satires of Sir David Lyndsay, which

> ' Branded the vices of the age,
> And broke the keys of Rome.'

After the martyrdom of George Wishart, Cardinal
Beaton was killed in the Castle of St. Andrews by the
Leslies of Rothes, with whom he had a business quarrel;
and associated with them were Kirkcaldy of Grange and
Melvill of Raith, the latter a friend of Wishart's, and
bent on avenging his death.   Cardinal Beaton be-
queathed his enormous wealth by will to his six natural
children.

In 1555 the Cardinal's house was rented by the city
for the temporary use of the Grammar School, while the
new High School was 'being biggit on the east side of
the Kirk of Field.'   The Edinburgh High School, though
not under the one roof, remained on the Blackfriars
ground for upwards of 270 years; but on the 23d June
1829, the boys, after giving three cheers to the old

H

memories, marched away four abreast to the new building on the Calton Hill. To the remanent members of
that day's leave-taking—a thinning band now, as the
years of the century are waxing old—there remain
pleasant and picturesque memories of the old High
School Wynd : the piazza house at the top, believed
then to be a Dutch house from Amsterdam, with its
wooden piles visible ; the dormer-windowed roofs ; the
queer timber outshots, sorely troubled with old age ; not
one house like its neighbour, but each possessing its
own artistic individuality, and ending with the Cardinal's
Tower standing boldly across the middle of the Wynd
at the foot.

That Tower was believed to be the model of a bottle-
shaped dungeon of traditional horrors in St. Andrews.
The 'Yairds'' wit, moreover, had named it 'Cardinal
Beaton's bluidie Peerie.' It must be confessed that the
similitude, when viewed from the High School Wynd,
was not unstriking ; and, to a High School boy, reverence in any matter connected with Cardinal Beaton
will ever be—an unknown quantity.

In 1562 the 'Cardinallis ludging in the Blak Freir
Wynd' was the scene of festivities consequent on the
marriage of the Earl of Moray to Lady Agnes Keith.
Queen Mary graced the feast, and was conveyed home
by 'honest young men of the toun in masqueing attire.'

In Cardinal Beaton's house, in the last quarter of the

eighteenth century, and under the sign of the Golden Cock, was a shop belonging to the last of the 'Lorimers,' a trade now extinct in name, but which, in the original seal of cause granted in 1483 to the Incorporation of Hammermen, ranked third on the roll. A Lorimer made the iron-work used by saddlers, and the word exists as a surname. Many of the old trades are surnames, as Fletcher (an arrow-maker), another extinct craft, Baker or Baxter, Sievwright, Goldsmith, Fuller, etc. The Gentle Reader can extend the list at will. It is a profitable pastime, and a pleasant.

A PROCESSION.

The Parliament Stairs and South Gable of the Old Parliament Hall.

THE Parliament Stairs, otherwise the Back Stairs, and the Meal Mercat Stairs, formerly had their steep ascent from the Cowgate up to the Parliament Close, which, since the first quarter of this century, has had its ancient name regrettably modernised into that of the Parliament Square—an infringement at once of the laws of Euclid and of good taste.

The Parliament Close was originally the churchyard belonging to the High Kirk of St. Giles. It extended down the steep slope to the Cowgate—the nether part being termed the Lower Kirkyard, or the Kirkheugh. On the Kirkheugh, near the site of the Parliament Stairs, once stood the Chapel of the Haly Rude, in which Walter Chepman endowed an altar with his tenement in the Cowgate, 1528. Walter Chepman, along with Andrew Myllar, was the first to introduce printing into Scotland (1507), under the sympathetic patronage and he occasional personal assistance of King James IV.

116

On the west side of the Parliament Close, prior to the Reformation, stood the houses of the Provost and the resident clergy of St. Giles.   These houses subsequently became the manses of the Protestant city ministers. In 1632, on the site which these buildings had occupied,

AN EARLY PRINTING-OFFICE.

was built the Parliament Hall—sometimes called the Westminster Hall of Scotland.   The oak ceiling beams, and the same fulness of roof space, are characteristic of the Scottish Parliament Hall, as they are of the Great

Hall of the Southern kingdom; and the memories of

OLD PARLIAMENT HOUSE AND STAIRS.

the historic past associated with both testify that the resemblance is that of kinship of spirit as well as that of kinship of form. The Parliament Hall was used exclusively for the meeting of the Scottish Parliament till the Union, which was consummated under its roof, 1st May 1707 —a measure then deemed by patriotic Scottish statesmen as a dark cloud and a frowning providence to Scotland, but to whose children the cloud's silver lining has come, bringing a prosperity of which their fathers never could have dreamed.

Since 1707 the Parliament Hall has been the abode of the Supreme Courts of Judicature for Scotland. The side wynd in the Old Edinburgh Exhibition terminates with a representation of the south gable of the Parliament Hall, which looked down on the steep stone stairs that led to the Cowgate. These stairs were removed in the changes that followed upon the Great Fire of 1824.

At the head of the Parliament Stairs in the Exhibition, and towards the left, there is a corridor, the open timber-work roof of which is a facsimile of that of the Old Hall at Linlithgow,—which was taken down so recently,—and which once belonged to the Knights Hospitallers of St. John of Jerusalem. So far as we know, there is only one open timbered oak roof now remaining in Scotland, namely, that at Darnaway Castle, Forres. The needless and almost wilful destruction of the Linlithgow Hospitium is a matter of irreparable regret.

The Assembly Rooms in the Bow.

A T the first angle of the Bow down from the Lawnmarket, and on the west side of the street, stood
the first Assembly Rooms,—a high, picturesque building,
and the last within the original city wall of James II.
The iron hook on which the Bow Port had swung
remained firmly batted into the wall of the house till
the old Bow street was practically swept away in 1836.
This building seems to have been erected by Peter
Somerville, a bailie of Edinburgh. His initials, the
arms of the Somervilles, the date 1602, and the motto
'IN DOMINO CONFIDO,' were carved on the architrave
of the door. In the first quarter of the present century
the premises were occupied by Mrs. Frier, a dealer[1] in

---

[1] When the Lawnmarket ceased to be the linen-market, and
home-spinning fell into disuse, the shop of this worthy lady was a
place where hand-woven linen might still be procured. For this she
appears to have had a select circle of *waiting* customers. The
Melrose carrier once brought a message from her to the mistress
of a Border farmhouse, to wit : ' Try and spare me a web or twa of
six or seven slip yarn. The Lord Advocate and Lord —— have
been here twice, and they are in sair need o' sarks ' !

wool, Galashiels grey,[1] and Scottish blankets.   One of

THE ASSEMBLY ROOMS IN THE BOW..

[1] In former days the staple manufacture of that prosperous burgh. To quote the words of an aged informant—dead since the above lines were written—'Galashiels grey was a maist durable claith, made o' sound woo', wi' a guid twined thread, and wairpit and weftit *wi' conscience.*' This being the case, one does not wonder at the durability nor—the prosperity.

the latter articles, known familiarly as a 'shearer's blanket,' flapping out at the window, did duty as a sign. Ascending by a turnpike stair, the second floor was reached, which, though subdivided in its latter days, had evidently at one time been a large and lofty room with panelled walls and a carved oak ceiling. A small room, formed by an outshot from the building, was a retiring-place, where the fiddlers, proverbially ' *drouthie,*' could

ROSINING THE BOW.

rosin their bows figuratively as well as literally. In 1710 the Revolution Whig party, under Godolphin and Sunderland, went into the temporary eclipse which ended with the death of Queen Anne. That child-bereaved queen, emancipated from the thraldom of the Duchess Sarah of Marlborough, and under the more suave guidance of Oxford and Mrs. Masham, was understood to favour the succession of her half-brother, the exiled Stewart Prince, rather than that of the more remote relative, as appointed by the Act of the Protestant

Succession. The Tory party in Edinburgh, synony-
mous at that time with Jacobitism, jubilant at finding
themselves once more in office and in the sunshine
of Court favour, held the first public dancing Assembly that same year. The innovation was not
regarded favourably in Edinburgh; and on one occasion the Assembly Rooms were assaulted, and the door
burned with red-hot spits. And yet the amusement
was somewhat severe. Ladies and gentlemen occupied
different parts of the room. Minuets and country
dances with silence
formed the pro-
gramme of the
evening,—at least
when under the eye
of the Lady Direc-
tress; but doubtless
that old story,
which is understood
to be the accom-
paniment of all such
gatherings, would
find some way of
being told. And
what a gay scene

MINUETS WITH SILENCE.

in the old Bow outside! Gilded sedan-chairs, velvet-
lined, with their liveried bearers, the fair occupants

attired in the dignified dress of the period—'gleam of satin and glimmer of pearl,' lace lappets, stately stomachers and trains, which in these days, be it noted, were *worn* and not trailed. The hours kept were early. The wave of the presiding dowager's fan was *Medo-Persianic*—the music was silent—the link-boys are ready with their torches—the gentlemen, in Ramillies

THE GENTLEMEN IN RAMILLIES WIGS.

wigs, velvet coats, lace Steinkirks, and wrist ruffles, sword at side and hat in hand, bow their fair partners to their chairs. They see them home — and the street is silent.

The Assemblies at first had a spasmodic existence in Edinburgh. About 1720 they were transferred to rooms in the Old Assembly Close. Oliver Goldsmith records his amusing description of these second Assembly Rooms in 1753, which were also the scene of the dignified but despotic reign of the famed Miss Nicky Murray.

Another amusement, affected by a more youthful section of Old Edinburgh, used to be carried on in the Bow. This was the ' Bickers,' made classical by Sir Walter Scott's self-recorded share in them, and by his story of ' Greenbreeks.' The Bow was the Thermopylæ of battle between the Grassmarket and West Port ' laddies ' on the one hand, and the Castlehill and Lawnmarket ' callants ' on the other. Down to the first ' bend ' it belonged to the ' High Toun,' and a line drawn from the Assembly Rooms across to the entrance of the close that led to Major Weir's house, of weird wizard fame, was as keenly assailed and as bravely defended as ever were the historical marches on the Borders between Scotland and England. Belted Will Howards and Bothwells of Hermitage were not wanting amongst the youthful wardens of the Bow marches. How the news spread that a ' bicker ' was to be ' on ' is best known to boy-nature, much the same in all ages ; but as the hour approached, boys, ' gentle and semple,' were to be seen hurrying to the rendezvous, armed with sticks or shinties, mostly in inverse ratio to the size of the warriors, and with pockets bulging with a select assortment of stones. There might be councils of war beforehand, but in face of the enemy the leader was autocratic. Obedience was an intuition ; prompt confiscation and social ostracism were the punishment of dissentients. If the Town Guard appeared upon the

scene, as it usually did in the fulness of time, there was
a swift coalition of all the belligerents against the com-

IF THE TOWN GUARD APPEARED.

mon enemy! The
bickers were danger-
ous both to life and
property, and it is
truly astonishing now
to note with what
equanimity the elder
citizens regarded the
matter, when as yet
police and plate-glass
were not. It was
their own children
and their neighbours'
who were fighting;
they were struggling as their fathers had done before
them; there might be some 'loźens' broken in the
windows;—the good house-mothers had some linen
rags and some simple 'heal-all' on a handy shelf;
nay, to this day grave and reverend seniors startle
one with tales of their prowess in the 'bickers' that
belonged to their own special neighbourhood, although
in their mature years they have never been overcome
by a temptation to rush out and give a helping hand,
as is the recorded feat of King James's friend, Tam
o the Cowgate, when Lord President of the Court

of Session ! [1]   It is related of Mr. Thomas Nelson, who occupied the Bow-head piazza shop, and who was

AS THEIR FATHERS HAD DONE BEFORE THEM.

the founder of the great publishing firm of Messrs. Thomas Nelson and Sons, that when one of these bickers seemed imminent, even in comparatively recent times, he said, 'Shut the shop, the lads maun hae their training ;'

[1] Sir Thomas Hamilton of Priestfield, Earl of Melrose 1619, and afterwards first Earl of Haddington 1627.

and after looking on for a while, with some other elderly citizens, who had a gleeful pinch of snuff over the

A GLEEFUL PINCH.

matter, he betook himself quietly home to his house in Trotter's Close, in the West Bow, while another sought his in Blair's Close in the Castle Hill. In this latter close was born, in 1757, Sir David Baird, of the Newbyth family, who, before he joined the British army, at the age of fifteen, to become the conqueror of Seringapatam and of Tippoo Sahib, won his first laurels as leader of a famous 'Bow bicker.' He drove the enemy, fighting all the way down the Bow, back through the Grassmarket to the West Port, and returned the same way. It may have been some of these doings which made his mother say, when she heard that Hyder Ali had chained the British prisoners one to the other in their captivity, ' Lord pity the lad that 's cheenyed to oor Davie !' It is worth stating, however, that the lad so 'cheenyed' lived to come home and tell that Davie was as tender to his comrade in distress, as he was terrible to his enemies in battle.

Our intimate acquaintance with the Bow and the Castle-Hill district is owing to a business connection which, for two lives prior to our own, existed with property in the latter street; the last tenement having been sold so late as 1855 to form Short's Observatory. Similar factorages—each a very coign of vantage for antiquarian observation, and differing much from casual visits—were held for houses in the High Street, the Canongate, the Grassmarket, Blackfriars Wynd, and last—but not least pleasant—with 'Old Newhaven.' Prior to the Irish immigration consequent on the construction of railways, which took place in the '*forties*,' the Castle Hill was tenanted mostly by a Celtic race. Being near the Castle, the tenants were chiefly old pensioners—long-service men who had fought in the Peninsular wars and at Waterloo.   Frasers and Frazers, Gordons and Grants, Camerons, M'Kenzies, and M'Donalds, are among the names we recall.   They eked out their pensions as chairmen and porters.

Our predecessors' experience did not tally with the character for dirt and poverty sometimes ascribed to the indwellers of these *lands*.   On the contrary, the houses were, as a rule, clean, 'bien,' and comfortable, but the counter complaints against antiquarian intruders were frequent, and sometimes amusing.

One of these old pensioners demanded a change of house.   He had been at a funeral, and was in the act

I

of resuming his working clothes, when a well-known antiquary—Charles Kirkpatrick Sharpe[1]—and two ladies,
without knocking, walked into his room.   Donald, equal
to the emergency, seized the bed-quilt, and improvised
a Highland kilt or a Roman toga on the spot.   ' " My
coot man," ' said the intruder—we give Donald's own
words,—a queer blend of heather English and the
home Doric of the Castle Hill,—" My coot man," said
he, " I hef procht two leddies to pe seen your lum and
ta carfings on it, and ta blue tiles," and ta two womans
stood like a kye, and tid not go out whatefer.   Now, Sir,
ta lum is a coot lum, and goes fery well, but—she wants
a shange.   She wants ta lum that she will put on ta
trews with teecency, with no carfings, and no " coot
mans." '   Donald got what he desired—a house with
an everyday chimney-piece.

Another tenant's description was even more graphic:
—'They are,' said she, 'weel-put-on men thae antick
folk, but sair gien to breakin' the tenth command, and
even wi' the *echt* I wadna like to lippen ower muckle to
their reverence.   They want to buy my pouther trenchers,
and ca' my hoose clean.   Hoo wad they like for me to
gang and ca' *their* hoose clean?   but maybe they ha'e
thae feckless, haundless, new-fashioned wives that ken
naething, no' like my mither's auld mistress, Leddy

---

[1] Well known in the literary world by his antiquarian writings,
and locally by his *sobriquet* ' Cheepin' Chairlie.'

Baird, wha cam doon the stair every Friday nicht, and passed a white lawn napkin ower the pan-shanks and the pot-bools to see that a' was clean and perfeck; and she had mair dignity in her auld backbane than wad ser' a' the New Toun o' Edinbro.   Puir bodies! I never like to hear *men* folk praisin' cleanliness.'

This old spinster possessed the only 'bink' of shining Scottish pewter trenchers we were ever privileged to see, a miniature of 'Sir Davie,' and a dress shoe of faded blue satin, a triumph of the 'cordiner's' skill, with a heel—we measured it with our first foot-rule—$2\frac{3}{16}$ inches high.   The Leddy Baird who had worn it, —perhaps at some of the old Assemblies,—must, like Queen Elizabeth, have danced—disposedly.

LORD PITY THE LAD.

The Black Turnpike.

THIS building was the second house west from the old Tron Church. It was taken down in 1788 for the carrying out of the plans consequent on the erection of the South Bridge, Sir James Hunter Blair being then the Lord Provost—from whom both Hunter Square and Blair Street take their names. It occupied the site of the present corner of the High Street and Hunter Square, and it was entered by three several turnpike stairs. It was of massive height and large extent, and had it not been disfigured by an inartistic timber front, it would have been, according to Maitland, one of the most sumptuous houses in Edinburgh. Tradition ascribed its erection to King Kenneth III. (994), but the above historian gives the date of a sasine (1461) in favour of George Robertson of Lockhart, the builder's son. There was, however, a later date (1674) over one of the doors in Peebles Wynd, doubtless that of some later alteration, with the legend—one of the most beautiful in the old city—

PAX INTRANTIBUS : SALUS EXEUNTIBUS.[1]

The ground-rents belong to George Heriot's Hospital.

[1] 'Peace to those who enter : safety to those who go out.'

In 1567 the Black Turnpike was the stately town house of Sir Simon Preston of that Ilk and Craigmillar, Provost of Edinburgh, and from its windows Queen Mary saw the last of her kingdom's capital. Alarmed by the exertions that Bothwell was making to secure her infant son James, and a reported speech to the effect that the young Prince

THE BLACK TURNPIKE.

would never live to ask him any questions as to his father's death, a party of the Scottish nobles arose in arms. Mary met them at Carberry, June 15, 1567, but her army melted away without drawing sword. She bade farewell to Bothwell on the bloodless field, surrendered herself to the Confederated Lords, and was brought that night a prisoner to the Provost's house at the Black Turnpike.

The character of Queen Mary is one of the vexed problems of history, and it will remain so, though the

weight of evidence seems now to be on the side of
those that believe in her guilt, however fain to have
it otherwise.

QUEEN MARY AND DARNLEY.

It was to a Protestant Scotland that Mary returned
from France in 1561, and, unlike her mother, she made
no open attempt to subvert the Reformed religion.
She asked, and barely received, toleration for the rites
of her own faith—already become unpopular.   The
blunder was in her marriage to Darnley, July 29, 1565,

against the advice of friend and foe. So strong was the
Guise opposition that it is said the Cardinal de Lorraine, an astute man of the world, would have concurred
in the substitution of the Huguenot Prince de Condé,
who had loved Mary from her youth. She preferred
the 'lang lad Darnley,' needy, greedy, dissolute—possessed of good looks, it is true, and of a knack of
writing love-songs; possessed, likewise, of a family
motto, AVANT DARNLÉ, JAMAIS D'ARRIÈRE,—to live up
to which he lacked moral vertebræ, and which motto
he made the text of every demand, from 'pooch
siller' up to the crown matrimonial. He was three
years younger than Mary, not out of his teens, and,
after her, the next heir to the Crown of England; but a
poor type in brain, heart, and courage of the powerful
races of Stewart, Tudor, and Douglas. Mary's power
of mind and strength of will have never been disputed.
Respect could not exist for Darnley, and love fled after
his share in the assassination of her secretary Rizzio.

Murray away, and Rizzio dead, Bothwell became her
chief counsellor. A loyal servant to the Queen he
appears to have been at first; and in the year 1566 he
was appointed Warden of the Three Marches, also
High Admiral, and obtained grants of the Abbeys of
Haddington and Melrose.

During the night between the 9th and 10th February,
1567, the citizens of Edinburgh were roused by the

noise caused by the blowing up of the Provost's house
of the Kirk-of-Field, and the next morning the body of

THE CITIZENS WERE ROUSED.

Darnley was found dead in the orchard adjoining. The
crime was Bothwell's. Whether Queen Mary knew
will possibly never be known, but existing doubts were
deepened by the history of Edinburgh that spring-time.
On April 12 Bothwell was nominally tried and acquitted.
On April 24, at the head of 1000 men, he intercepted

the Queen on her road from Stirling at Foullbrigs (now
Fountainbridge), near Edinburgh, and conducted her
prisoner to Dunbar.   On May 7 he was divorced from
his young wife, Lady Jean Gordon, whom he had married fourteen months before.   On May 12 he was created
Duke of Orkney, and on the 15th of the same month
Mary married him—a weariful fact, for which no justifi-
cation can be found, and which practically dethroned
her; hence the confederacy of the nobles, the unfought
battle of Carberry, the revilings of the people; and
hence the banner representing the young Prince praying
for vengeance beside the dead body of his father, that
met her weeping gaze as she looked down on the High
Street the next morning from the window of the Black
Turnpike.

 This was no fight of rival religions.   Bothwell was a
Protestant, and had helped well to get all the Church
lands in Edinburgh gifted by charter to the city.   The
quarrel was as old as royalty itself—the safety of the
seed-royal. The Scottish people, inherently loyal, turned
to the child.   With them it was: 'What of the bonny
Duke of Rothesay, starved to death at Falkland by his
uncle Albany?' and 'What of these fair young Planta-
genet Princes, Edward and Richard of York, who, only
eighty years before, had passed into the Tower of
London and were never heard of more?'   The women
of Edinburgh have come under blame, as to their speech

and conduct, at this juncture. It is to be remembered, however, that we see Mary's history through the softened gloom of her unlawful imprisonment and her unrighteous death; but to the citizens of Old Edinburgh the roar of that Sabbath at midnight was in their ears, and the thought of that 'ower sune step-faither' sent the mothers of the High Street and the Canongate 'from their bairnis cradellis to ban.'

The next day Mary crossed the Firth of Forth to Loch Leven. A year passed, and then came the gallant deliverance from the island castle, the gathering of the Setons and the Hamiltons to her help, the defeat of Langside, and the far ride to the Solway sands. Not to France for refuge, not to Catherine de Medicis, whom she had flouted as a merchant's daughter—but to Elizabeth and England, for sympathy, succour, protection, and redress. She crossed the Solway to England and Elizabeth, and at her hands—the hands of the Queen of England—she received captivity, death, and a grave.

In both countries the influence of the age was towards good. It was the birth-time of motive forces that have levered the world on to the lines of religious, social, and intellectual rectitude and progress—the endeavours of both Crown and people, working steadily and sternly, though often blindly, to issues greater than they knew; but in these there is no apology for sin, no palliation—none. For *that* pardon may have been sought, and pardon found; but in the fierce light that beat on these rival thrones, and that was reflected and flashed back from south to north, and from north again to south, we read with silent and reverent pitifulness —how sore a thing it was to be a Queen.

THE FAR RIDE TO THE SOLWAY SANDS.

The Cowgate House fornent the Mint Close.

THIS house stood on the south side of the Cowgate, and in the earlier years of its existence it was one of the timber-fronted burgher dwellings, with a piazza on its ground floor and an open gallery on the floor above. This fashion of house-building gave a safe open-air play-nook for the children, and a pleasant place for the old people to sit in the sun. The interior, however, of these dwellings must have been very dark. The windows of Edinburgh down to the Restoration had only the upper sash glazed, and this sash was a fixture. The under half consisted of folding shutter-boards, which were open in fine weather, and closed during the storms and cold of winter. These shutters were of all qualities, from plain 'eastland buirds' up to carved oak. In business we have passed these short shutter-panels through our hands richly carved on both sides—that is, adorned to the inside of the house as well as to the outside. In one instance the carved oak

was framed round brasses exquisitely chased.   These
burnished brasses, which were fitted to the window with

curiously made cen-
tre-pin hinges, be-
sides adding to the
beauty of the in-
terior, would aid
materially in light-
ing it up.

We have already
noted that the reign
of James I. was the
birth-time of many
of the Scottish
manufactures.   In
1610 that of glass
was begun at

COWGATE HOUSE.

Wemyss, in Fife, while those of potash and 'saip' (soap)
had their earliest days in Leith, under Patrick Maule,
said to be the founder of the family of Panmure.   The
glass at first was coarse, and abounded in the thick,
green-tinted 'yolks' once so common, but which have
well-nigh disappeared since rolled plate has superseded
blown glass.

When this Cowgate house was in process of being
taken down, we visited it more than once, when out
on antiquarian rambles with the late James Drum-

mond, R.S.A. We found one back window with the original upper transom, to which an under sash.of later workmanship had been added. The former was of oak, with strong finely-moulded and wrought astragals, and, as a specimen of joiner work, *perfect.* This was one of the oldest houses in the Cowgate, and contemporary with that of Symson the printer. Its windows must have faced the winters and the summers of more than three hundred and fifty years, but not one of these mitres had been 'guttered' in the cutting, not a joint was started, and a stone had to be displaced before it could be removed, which perhaps accounted for its remanent solitariness. The worthy brother of the good 'Wrycht Craft' of St. Mary's Chapel who made it—saw or chisel could not be lifted in the city out of the guild—had nothing to learn from the improved tools of modern days. This transom window was added to Mr. Drummond's own collection. Nothing certain is known of the 'indwellers' of this house.

The Town Guard.

FROM the time of Flodden (1513) onwards, companies of soldiers were embodied at various times to guard the city; but the embodiment proved always temporary, and the watching and warding invariably returned into the hands of the citizens. In 1625 each citizen took his turn of martial duty every twenty-fifth night. The last disbandment was of a company of 108 men, who had been raised at the instigation of the Duke of York, and was commanded by Captain Patrick Grahame, the Magistrates having petitioned the Estates to the effect 'that the common prison and private men's shops had been more frequently broken since the raising of the said companie than before'! The citizens did not take kindly to the return to night-watching, and shortly afterwards the Town Guard is found formally established, and the low, long, one-storied dingy guard-house built in the middle of the High Street esplanade.

The picture by Kay of this house is well known, with the fierce Corporal John Dhu looking over the shut

half-door, and the wooden horse, with its peculiarly
acute-angled back, standing at the western gable. This
animal, otherwise known as the 'trie meir,' must have
been a terror to evil-doers in the corps and elsewhere.
If a soldier was disguised in liquor, or was guilty of
using opprobrious language, or was absent from his
duty on guard-day, by the rules of the service he for-
feited two days' pay—6d. per diem—and had to ride

RIDING THE WOODEN HORSE.

the wooden horse for one hour,—a punishment aggra-
vated by muskets being bound to the soles of the
culprit's feet. The solitary and suffering unit excepted,
it must have been beyond the power of human nature
to resist a smile.

Entry into the City's service, however, was eagerly
sought by the returned Highland soldiers who had seen
foreign service. The Town Guard-house was taken

down in 1785, after which the city corps occupied one
of the Tolbooth shops facing the Luckenbooths.   The
'Toon Rats,' or 'Rattens,' as they were named, were the
natural and hereditary enemies of the youth of the old
city, and of plenty who had left their youth behind, but
who retained its frolics and its follies.   To the former
belonged the poet, poor Fergusson, who evidently was
acquainted with the 'Black Hole' below the 'flags' of
the captain's room in the Town Guard-house.

> ' And thou, great god o' aqua-vitæ,
> Wha sways the empire o' this city,
> When fou we 're sometimes capernoity ;
>   Be thou prepared
> To hedge us frae that *black banditti*,
>   The City Guard.
>
>   .   .   .   .   .
>
> O soldiers ! for your ain dear sakes,
> For Scotland, alias *Land o' Cakes*,
> Gie not her bairns sic deidly paiks,
>   Nor be sae rude
> Wi' firelock and Lochaber aix,
>   As spill their blude.'

On the adoption of the modern Police system, and
the consequent disbandment of the Town Guard in
1817, a sinecure guardianship of the Parliament Close
was accorded by the Lord Provost and Council to John
Kennedy, a private in the City Corps.   Old, bent, and
shrivelled—and ever carrying his Lochaber axe—he
ceased not for years to pace, or rather, latterly, to totter

round the statue of Charles II. A faithful terrier, in appearance equally aged, was long his companion. With John Kennedy died the last, in office, of the Town Guard of Edinburgh.

The Janitor and Officers in the Old Edinburgh of the Exhibition are dressed in the garb of the Town Guard.

THE LAST GUARDSMAN.

The Blue Blanket and the Trades Incorporations.

TRADITION places the origin of the Blue Blanket, the Trades Banner of Edinburgh, in the twelfth century. Scottish craftsmen followed Allan, Lord High Steward of Scotland, to the Holy Land in the third Crusade, when Richard Cœur de Lion, the hero of Christendom, was matched against Saladin, the champion of Moslem chivalry. The Scottish banner was inscribed with this legend from Psalm li., 'In bona voluntate tua edificentur muri Ierusalem—'In thy good pleasure let the walls of Jerusalem be built.' The craftsmen bore the flag honourably in battle, brought it home, and dedicated it to the altar of St. Eloi, their patron saint, in the High Kirk of St. Giles. It was styled the Banner of the Holy Ghost, but was familiarly and fondly known from its colour as the Blue Blanket.

The full story is given in a quaint old book written in 1722 by Alexander Pennicuik, Guild brother of Edinburgh. The author magnifies his office, and proves, to his own satisfaction, that the Trades should take precedence of the Professions, inasmuch as hand labour was the occupation of Adam and Eve in a state of innocence, while the professions of Divinity, Law,

and Physic were the result of the Fall, which was caused
by the intervention of the devil !

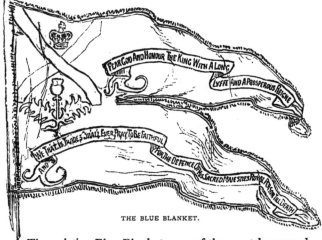

THE BLUE BLANKET.

The existing Blue Blanket, one of the most honoured
relics of Scottish antiquity—it was brought back from
Flodden Field—and of which the Incorporated Trades
of Edinburgh are the guardians, was a gift in 1482 from
James III. and his Queen, Margaret of Denmark, who
worked it with her own hands.   At the unfurling of the
banner, not only the craftsmen of Edinburgh, but every
burgher craftsman in the country, is bound to obey the
summons, 'weil bodin in feir of weir,' under the command of the Convener of the Edinburgh Trades.[1]

[1] 'Ilk Burges hauand fyftie pundis in gudis salbe haill anarmit,
as a gentilman aucht to be : . . . and Burgessis of xx pund in

The character of James III. as a social reformer
repays close investigation better than that of the more
brilliant sovereigns of his race.   He seems to have set
before himself the problem of raising the citizen or
burgher power to act as a counterpoise to the feudal
arrogance of the nobles.   Markets for different goods
were systematised, their times and places regulated, a
public weigh-house was established for the first time,
and in the seventh year of his reign the National Scottish Fisheries were begun, a measure which in itself alone
stamps nobility on the mind that originated it.   Old
Edinburgh benefited largely : the Provost was made hereditary sheriff within his own town ; the magistrates and
council were empowered to make bye-laws and statutes
for its good government ; duties on necessary commo-
dities were rescinded ; and the Incorporation charters,
with very few exceptions, date from this reign.   Reading these old charters, or 'Seals of Cause,' one by one,
there comes to the mind a large respect for the wisdom
and thoroughness of both King and Craftsmen, and a
suspicion that Archibald Bell-the-Cat, Earl of Angus,
when he hanged the royal favourites over Lauder
Bridge, aimed at the throttling of the King's measures
fully as much as the death of the King's men.

The Edinburgh Incorporated Trades of the Mag-

gudis salbe bodin with hat, doublet or habirgeoun, sword and
bucklar, bow, scheif and knyfe.'—Acts Jas. I. 1429, c. 137.   Edit.
1566, c. 123, Murray.

dalen Chapel are the Goldsmiths,[1] Skinners, Furriers, Hammermen (17 companies), Wrights, Masons (these last two are named the Associated Trades of St. Mary's Chapel, with 10 companies), Tailors, Baxters, Fleshers, Cordiners, Websters, Waukers, and Bonnet-makers. Then follow the Candlemakers and several of the smaller crafts. Each Corporation possesses its own armorial bearings, and these blazonries are represented in the Exhibition. The Blue Blanket is fitly and safely guarded in the Trades Maiden Hospital. Its duplicate floats over 'Old Edinburgh.'

[1] The surgeons, associated with the barbers, were formerly the first of the crafts, but were dissociated 1657.

RETURN FROM FLODDEN.

The Cross.

IF King James VI. styled his canonised ancestor, David I., a 'sair sanct for the Croun,' there is as little doubt that, during his own occupancy of the Scottish throne, he was for Edinburgh a *sair sorner on the toun*. The Provost and the 'Thesaurer' must have felt many a sinking of heart over the frequent royal missives with the superscription 'Traist Freindis, we greitt zow [1] weill,' and the signature 'James R.'

By these letters the town was ordered to entertain royal and national guests, and that for any amount of time— as the Danish Ambassador, the Dutch, the Venetian, and the French Ambassadors; the daughters of the Duke of Lennox (there was some grumbling at this); but the Duke of Holstein, the Queen's brother, was feasted 'with great solemnitie and mirrines.' Accord-

[1] The letter 'z' in the old Scots language is pronounced 'y;' thus Cunzie House is pronounced Cunyie House, and Mackenzie— Mackenyie.

ing to Maitland, the money due by the King to the city was 59,000 merks, but the civic council was obliged to take 20,000 merks as full payment. Not-

withstanding all this, and in spite of his endless interference in their elections, there was a kindly feeling between James and his Edinburgh subjects. The good city, like Issachar of old, saw that rest was good and the land that it was pleasant, and it certainly bowed its shoulder to bear, and became a servant unto tribute ; but the same year

THE CROSS.

that saw James, the King of England gave Edin- burgh its Golden Charter. By it 'the King deter- mined to leave to the citizens a perpetual monument to posterity, and, as a token for future ages, his Majesty not only ratified all its previous charters and ancient immunities and privileges, but invested it with greater and higher privileges beyond all the burghs and cities of his Dominion.'[1]   The whole charter, in fact, reads more like a benediction, or rather a presentation speech, than a legal State document.

In the High Street, on April 5, 1603, taking a weeping farewell of his tearful Queen and of his mourning people—who foresaw and dreaded the evils of Court absenteeism,—James set out with no small pageantry to his new kingdom.   The tears of prosperity are sweet, and they are soon dried.

The 'Mercat Croce,' from which he had been proclaimed in his infancy, and which he left behind him on that day of farewells, is *the* Cross represented in the 'Old Edinburgh' of the Exhibition.   Fourteen years afterwards (1617), this Cross was taken down and rebuilt on a different site in the High Street, as part of the preparations in honour of James's expected return to visit his 'auncient kingdom.'   He came also to a new Nether-Bow Port, and to the restored Palaces of Holyrood, Stirling, and Falkland.   Not only so, but the burghs of Scotland undertook to feed and furnish an assessed number of cattle as *vivers* for their King and his train of courtiers.   The method of rating seems strange to the present day.   The city of Glasgow and the burgh of Dundee provided each 300 fed nolt (nowt); Brechin 100; Perth 60; Musselburgh 12; Newbattle 30; the

[1] Inventory of Selected Charters and Documents from the Charter-House of the City of Edinburgh, 1884, p. 21.

town of Alloway 30; Montrose 36; Pittenweem 10: and Stirling '20 ky and 20 viellis.'[1]

King James came, was joyously welcomed at the West Port, and was 'propynit' with 10,000 merks in gold angels, contained in a silver gilt basin, which he received with 'ane myld and gracious countenance.' There the King saw the Magistrates and Council of Edinburgh in their first robes of office, with the city sword in its velvet sheath, for which, to put Edinburgh on a par with London, he had passed another special charter 1609—gifting the city, moreover, with two sable-trimmed robes by way of pattern. His Majesty then listened to a thanksgiving sermon in the High Kirk, knighted the Provost, William Nisbet of Dean, at St. John's Cross in the Canongate, and then once more passed below the roof-tree of his old home at Holyrood. James remained fifteen months in his northern kingdom, and thence returned to London, with an abundance of experiences and news to speak over with his gossip, George Heriot, as to how graciously Scotland had welcomed him—'even your awin native-born Prince, Geordie.'

The Cross which King James saw on that day of rejoicing, and which was removed in 1756, is that which has been restored to Edinburgh by the graceful

[1] Documents relative to the Reception at Edinburgh of Kings and Queens of Scotland, p. 103.

gift of Mr. Gladstone. Its shaft and capital formed part of the ancient Edinburgh Cross. Four of the original sculptured medallions of the same old Cross were built into the tower named ' Ross's Folly,' erected in the grounds of St. Bernard's, Stockbridge. Walter Ross had bargained with the Magistrates for some stones, but, getting up early one morning, he carted away the medallions instead. A correspondence ensued, but the medallions were never returned. According to his dying instructions, his body lay unburied for eight days, and thereafter the ' Folly ' became its owner's grave.

In 1824, after the death of Sir Henry Raeburn, who was the next owner of St. Bernard's, the tower was taken down for feuing purposes, and the medallions were given to Sir Walter Scott. Their removal from Ross's Folly was witnessed by Mr. Cumberland Hill when a boy. The heavy stone carvings were loosened by the masons, and fell softly, each into a separate cart that was backed against the tower. There had been many discussions between Tom Purdie and Sir Walter as to the transit; but what was the amusement and delight of the latter, when the four carts drew up before the Castle Street house, to find that Tom had filled them with stable manure!

Sir Walter and Sir Adam Ferguson went down into the street, bareheaded and laughing, to see the stones, and to ask explanations.

'What made you think of such a thing?' said Sir
Walter.

WHAT MADE YOU THINK OF SUCH A THING?

'Ye'll never get these real bits of the true Cross clean
again from that stuff, Tom,' added Sir Adam.

'Dinna fear,' replied Tom; 'it's saft, but no' sappy.
The notion jist cam into my heid like inspirawtion
last nicht when I was half-sleepin'. I never had muckle
broo o' thae new-fangled imitation manures, ye ken;
and it's no' easy doin' justice to oor land wi' half yin's
stable in Embro a' the winter. So, as there's nae gettin'

muck the noo in a' Muiris Pairish for either love or
siller, it was a twice lucky thocht to tak' this. It's far
better than the ait strae ye spak o', Sir Walter, for it will
carry oot the bits o' images as saft as a babby in a
blanket, and spread on Lauchie's haugh after a', and
that's fellin' twae dowgs wi' ae bane, and birlin' your
bawbee to come up baith heids and tails at yince ; mair
betoken, it didna cost ye a penny, for I got it oot o'
your ain toon stable yont the gait. As for Sir Awdam's
cleanin', when our Tweed rins dry, we'll aiblins speel
up the brae to his bit Huntley burn !'

Both gentlemen shook hands with Tom : ' Mind and
take a rest and a feed to yourselves and the horses at
Welsh's,'[1] cried Sir Walter ; and away went the carts
round the corner of George Street, up the steep
Liberton Brae, down the Gala Water road, then
in the full glory of the four-in-hand coaching days
of the Royal Mail—the Blucher and the Chevy-
chase—past Borthwick Castle, and Torsonce, and
Stow to Abbotsford. It was the last year of Sir
Walter's happiness before his misfortunes and his sorrows came.

Reading the inscription on the restored Cross, it
would have been better if these medallions had rejoined
the old pillared shaft and capital ; and it is not too

[1] ' Welsh's '—a famous roadside inn for carters, not far from
Fushiebridge.

much to say that, had the master mind that created
Abbotsford been alive, they would have come back to
Edinburgh, though not perhaps in the same fashion as
that in which they left it, and the malison which the
poet pronounced upon the iconoclasts of 1756 would
have been lifted.

The removal of the ancient buildings of Edinburgh
has its necessary and its unnecessary side. The driving
of ventilating side-shaft streets through the serried masses
of the densely crowded closes was necessary for the
health, the morality, and the well-being of the people.
The Civic Rulers of the city have hitherto regulated
wisely the momentum of these great measures, and in
this matter it becomes the most æsthetic lover of the
Past to yield to the philanthropist without a sigh.

As to the unnecessary side—the wanton destruction
of such erections as the 'Mercat Croce' is the very 'super-
fluity of naughtiness,' and for such procedure there is
no blame too heavy.   Maitland,[1] whose valuable folio
History was published in 1753, and who was the expon-
ent and mouthpiece of the Taste of the period, deliber-
ately wrote down the Market Cross.   Of the High
Street he thus speaks: 'This beautiful street is so
crowded and pestered with a Diversity of Edifices—the
Public Wells, the Market Cross, *a Building that may
well be spared*, it being only a Receptacle for Filth and

[1] Maitland, p. 216; also p. 183.

Nastiness . . . whereby its (the street's) beauty is greatly eclipsed.' Maitland is not the first man, nor will he be the last, that will lecture constituted authorities on matters of taste—and lead them wrong. Once and again he returns to the charge. The public mind was sedulously educated to believe in a boundless contiguity of *space*, and in three years (1756) the Cross fell. Apart from this act of immolation, let it be gently remembered that to Old Edinburgh, in these earliest years of the reign of George III., space and breathing-room must have seemed alike pleasant and beautiful. The old Flodden City Wall, though its bastions and towers had long been falling into decay, had still its boundaries respected; and for 250 years the city had increased only by the closest packing of her buildings, or by adding to their already over-towering height.

The next decade of that monarch's reign saw New Edinburgh born.

> ' Dun-Edin ! oh, how altered now !
> Where safe amid thy mountain court
> Thou sitt'st, like Empress at her sport,
> And liberal, unconfined, and free,
> Flinging thy white arms to the sea.'

The Book of Old Edinburgh is done, and the Past glides into the Present.

> ' Cloth of Gold do not despise
> Though thou be matched with Cloth of Frieze,
> Cloth of Frieze be not too bold
> Though thou be matched with Cloth of Gold.'

Which is the Gold and which is the Frieze? In the Past, as in the Present, there were both, and their union was STRENGTH in the history of Scotland—the fine gold of Intellect, the pure gold of Genius, the beaten wrought gold of Invention, and the strong-fibred, firmly-twined frieze threads of Labour.

Let them still continue to be blended and interwoven, and with them the heart loyalty of all sorts and conditions of men to their Country and their Sovereign, in humble dependence, but with lofty faith in that Power above, who has guided and blessed the Past, who alone rules in the Present, and who will direct and guard the Future of our beloved land!

THE END.

For EU product safety concerns, contact us at Calle de José Abascal, 56–1°,
28003 Madrid, Spain or eugpsr@cambridge.org.

www.ingramcontent.com/pod-product-compliance
Ingram Content Group UK Ltd.
Pitfield, Milton Keynes, MK11 3LW, UK
UKHW012342130625
459647UK00009B/469